T0194948

THE
MAKING *of a*
RENAISSANCE
MAN

BRIAN WILLETT

authorHOUSE®

AuthorHouse™
1663 Liberty Drive
Bloomington, IN 47403
www.authorhouse.com
Phone: 1 (800) 839-8640

Published by AuthorHouse 06/18/2019

ISBN: 978-1-7283-1630-7 (sc)
ISBN: 978-1-7283-1629-1 (e)

Library of Congress Control Number: 2019908060

Print information available on the last page.

Dedicated to my wife, children, and
Grandchildren, Andrew and Amy
Love Grandpa

Contents

If you are lucky during your life, you will experience a variety of activities, relationships, mentors, and passions, both good and bad; they should take pleasure in these. Take it from me and remember, "The day you are born, you start to die, **so make the most of it!"**

My life has been like a diamond made up of a number of different facets combined to give my life its' own unique brilliance. A man should be made up from a combination of skills in different areas such as being an artist, thinker, dreamer, and knowledgeable in different subjects. I want to forewarn the youth of today that they are missing out on different facets of life's rich experiences and the ability to use reason and resources to shine like a diamond. Hopefully, from reading my memoirs, I will enlighten some young people and adults to explore these vast treasures in this world and help them to enrich their lives, and also, I invite people my own age to enjoy reliving some of their youth through my unique stories. I didn't hold back or censor my words and feelings, so, fasten your seatbelts!

I will start by telling you about my variety of riches and experiences I have had in my life growing up in New England. My motto throughout my life has been, "Never say never unless you try." I've achieved this with a positive and confident attitude; sometimes I succeeded and others times I didn't, but it was always a worthwhile experience because I tried! I know for a fact that when you read these memoirs you will be saying, "This can't be happening to him!", "What now!", "I don't believe this!", "Unbelievable!" Well, they did happen and I survived to be a much richer man than if none of these events took place. I invite you to discover these avenues I have taken in reaching my state as a 'Renaissance Man.'

Chapter 1

FAMILY

MY MOTHER

I'm going to begin this book with my mother because this is where everyone's story begins! I always say, once a mother, always a mother. Let's begin this story in 2014, my mother was 90 years old and typically spent her days sitting in her comfy easy chair watching her TV with the volume up HIGH, while wondering in her head how her boys are doing. Being such a worrywart, her highlight for the day is to speak to each of her sons. Mom, having a lot of time to fantasize about what we are doing and how we are, dwells on why we haven't called her yet. As you'll learn from reading this book, she has always placed us boys first before her own needs.

For years, to occupy her day when she gets bored watching western TV shows and she reads a book a day. Lately, it has tapered off since she had to switch to large-print versions. There is nothing seriously physically wrong with her. She has a nurse come every month to take her vitals and has many friends stop in to chat and do errands for her. My daughter Cinda always sends her jokes in the mail so she can perform for her visitors. This gives Mom a new repertory of cute jokes or a story to share with them as soon as they come through her door!

Mom has been my mentor, ally, and best friend. I don't know what I would have done without her. I feel, she being a stay-at-home mom, provided us three boys with such an advantage. She comforted, cuddled, and protected me more than my other brothers because I was her smallest and least-healthy son. She singled me out by introduced me to all kind of life's opportunities and adventures to build me up and protected me from one's that could hurt me. I applaud Mom for keeping things from my father, or easing into them, to protect me.

My mother has been the most practical person in my life. She always had a place for everything, wrote to-do list, and organized her affairs ahead of time. She never ceased to amaze me when she could remember the smallest detail from her youth so she could share these details today with us boys. She was a good partner for my father because she helped managed his modest income and made our money go further. Since my father has been dead for over 30 years and my mother has lived 18 years in an HUD housing community, I drove almost two hours one way every week to do her errands and chores and to be a companion for her; my brother David does the same but not as often. Mom has always been here for us boys and us for her.

Well, in 2015, Mom's attitude and personality had drastically gone downhill. We went to visit Mom in February and she was sitting in her chair, unable to move, get up to eat, or go the bathroom. Her legs were swelled up twice their normal size. We called the ambulance and they took her to the hospital. Well, to make a long story a little shorter, she stayed for three days in the hospital and we decided to place her in the local nursing home where my wife Lavinia works. It's only ¼ mile away from our house and we can visit 3-4 times a day. I am heartbroken over this situation. But, life goes on

I really miss having those heart to heart talks over the phone we had several times a week. She would update me with the events taking place at her apartment complex; tell me what books she were reading with a full description; give me a shopping list for her supplies and, tell me to drive safely when I come over. On the way home from her place, I was required to call her as I approached my home so she would not worry about my travels. Heaven forgive me if I was late to call or the line was busy. These events have been going on for 18 years or more. But now, she's changed...she can't remember anything, not knowing why she is where she is, and has a limited thought process and confined in a wheel chair. She asks me if she had eaten, took her medicine, or went to the bathroom. She won't watch TV or answer the phone if it rings. Recently, being a thoughtful son, I have rekindled her musical abilities, by having her play her keyboard with one finger. If you name a song for her, or hummed it, she can play it! Also, I have introduced her back to playing cards, Rummy and Crazy 8's. She still struggles with Rummy, but I feel she will catch on. I keep my fingers 'crossed'! But, I'm glad that I had so many quality years, 65 years, with my mother. Now it is time for me to take care of her. Let me tell you about her beginning.

She was born in 1923 and she was named after her great, great aunt, Ann Tripp. Mom grew up in Belfast, Maine during the twenties, thirties and forties when there was war and rationing going on. When Dad came back from the service, he had to meet his new son Aiden and create a relationship with him who proved to be awkward for all because of his separations and his presents of PTSD.

I believe a person becomes stronger when they are shaped by events that only fate can control. It's odd how fate has its own 'way' of changing people's lives. Often, I wonder if there is a higher power in charge of our destinies; like we are a marionette and something else is pulling our life's strings!

Well Mom, at the young age of 20 years old, gave birth to her first son, Aiden. Unknown to her, because she was on another planet with the newness and complexity of giving birth on that day, her 15-years-old brother, Rob, was accidentally shot while hunting, and was killed. Do you believe that? My mother was very close to Rob, being only five years older, and raised him like her son while her parents worked at their store. While she was in the hospital, feeling devastated, sad and lonely, her mind was going in all directions. She thought to herself, "Why Rob?" "How could this happen today of all days when I have so much newness, joy and excitement to share with my family!" After trying to sort out the day's events, she came up with a solution. Being such a special daughter, she decided to offer her new-born son to her mother to replace her mother's loss and void. This actually didn't happen, but, as a result of the accident, my mother never had the joy and happiness of sharing her son's birth with her family and others. She must have thought everyone abandoned her until she heard about the tragedy. She must have cried her eyes out. Fate again aligned Rob's birthday with my birthday, which is January 9th. In honor of her brother Rob, my given middle name is Rob! I just found out yesterday, 72 years after Rob was shot, his favorite song was, You Are My Sunshine... Mom played it on her keyboard today for me and recalled this story.

To more understand my mother's dedication and the quality of her love towards her immediate family and her sons, I would like to share a recent loving experience. After me having a job for the past five years out of seven years, I became unemployed. It's a pain in the butt to apply for unemployment these days. You have to go to classes and seminars, apply to 3-5 jobs a week, and go to interviews. Knowing this, Mom felt awful bad that I hadn't had an interview during this jobless two-year spell, but then, I finally got an interview! My mom, being excited that I may finally get a job, called me several times to wish me luck with the interview. In the mean time, without me knowing, my mother secretly wrote a wish note and folded it up to a small size, and stuck it in her bra next to her heart for two days while all this stuff was going on. The note said: "Please, oh please, God, let Sandy get this job. All his life he has had trials...let him get this job-he can do it. I ask this in your name, Jesus the Savior!" When I found all this out, it made me cry that she used her 'mother's powers' to support my ventures! Now that's the power of this wonderful person, a genie, a mother and supporter behind me! Well, I never got a job so I decided to take my social security early at 62. This turned out to be a good choice and, a wonderful gift, giving me more quality time for myself and more time to spend with MOM! She always reminded me that, "I'm still full of piss and vinegar!" Her father was also!

Just a note to my readers: Your mother brought you into this world. She sacrificed, went without, cuddled, supported, urged, educated, and loved you for who you were; her son or daughter. There will be a day or a time when your mother isn't around either physically or mentally. I'm finding this out now...SO, cherish every moment with her. Spend quality time, and share secret thoughts or worries with her; she can take it. After all, we only have "ONE MOTHER!" I'm sorry; this last sentence brings tears to my eyes!

Deep breath, let's shift ahead to 2016. Mom has been in a nursing home for over one and a half years. During this time, Mom came up with a chant: It was, "Roses are red and violets are blue, and angel in heaven knows that I love you!" As she got closer to her end, she added, "And scissors Too!" To her, this was her tool to be able to cut her bonds from this earth and be able to enter heaven to be with her family!

"What I'm going to tell you next was totally unbelievable for us to whiteness!" While Mom was near her end, unconsciously while laying in her bed, she repeatedly reached her left arm out to the corner of the window sill and wall, then, grabbing and turning an imaginary knob, she retracted her arm back after making this motion as turning the knob of the door to Heaven and opening it to make her finally journey. This made us feel relieved that she finally made the journey. We covered her body with the wonderful blanket my daughter made for her with the pictures of all her grandchildren so she could take the journey with them and they would protect her. She passed three days before her 93thd birthday, Mom died with me and my wife at her side to the end.

When I called my brother David, his wife Diane, and our son Cedric to notify them that Mom was very close to the end they couldn't think what to say. We sat with her for hours and finally at 5:30 she took her last breath, then at 5:45 her heart finally stopped. My wife Lavinia and I, decided to perform Mom's post mortem care instead of a stranger, and the staff granted our wish. We washed her up with warm water and rose water and covered her while Lavinia washed and blow dried her hair. She chose her flowered purple top and her purple pants as her final outfit, as purple, was her favorite color. We put on her cozy blue socks to keep her feet warm for her journey and her black, shinny sparkly hat and her glasses on, Lavinia put make-up on her face and placed her glasses on, Even as I'm remembering this, Sorry I'm crying telling this story... We placed a bouquet of yellow, black- eyed Susans in her hands and placed her bible on her. Inside the bible were pictures of all of us with our names that said we all loved her and her chant; "Roses are red, Violets are blue, Angels in Heaven know I love you," "And scissors Too!" She finally looked relieved and at peace with herself. No more pain and agony. She is finally home and this is where she wanted to be for a long time. Now she can see her Papa, Mama, and son Aiden... tears are flowing again, Rob and her other brothers and sister.

The man from the funeral parlor came to pick up Mom and I met him and helped him with the gurney. I found out his name was Sandy and his mother's name was Elizabeth and he had red hair and a Trip-like face and movement. I wonder if he was a relative or an angel! Then, Lavinia mentioned that she had taken care of his wife's when she was a patient at the nursing home some 20 years ago when she was a LNA. This was very comforting for us. "We are going to miss you Mom!!!"

MY FATHER

My father was a typical boy while growing up in the '20s, having his share of boyhood adventures. He always told this story to us boys when we sat around an open fire so we wouldn't have the same bad experience he had had. "As a young boy, I was playing with fire and it got out of control. I tried to put it out by stomping on it, but the fire caught my trousers on fire, burning my leg severely below my knee. It was the worst pain I had ever felt as a young boy!" Dad never talked about this in detail, but I could see the pain and emotions in his eyes as he shared this life-changing experience. Knowing his family situation where he couldn't share his pain or love, I could see his pain being released as he warned us, "Never play with fire!" Whenever we built fires with the Boy Scouts, Dad's voice always internally cautioned us boys about the harm fire could cause.

When Dad was bad, which I understand was often, he was sent to the hot, isolated attic, where he opened up the small round window on the western eve to let air in and let the heat out, but most importantly called to his friends, He would drop down a string with a note on its end and some change, asking his friends to get things for him at the store while he was in isolation. In my mind, I can see him now opening this window and calling out to his friend Peewee, "Get me five Tootsie Rolls at Bacon's store. I'm hungry! Take this nickel wrapped in the note to buy them," "Hurry!" Mom always reminded me that's dad's nickname was "Tootsie" because of his fondness for Tootsie Rolls.

My father was brought up in an unhappy, stricter ruled home without love or affection. When growing up, I visited grandma's place as a child, I never saw any emotions expressed except, anger.

Between WWI and WWII, when life was not so lucrative and one had to save, they scrimped on food, saved everything for a rainy day, never went out to eat, or wasted food. His father made shoeboxes in the local shoe factory for the war efforts during WWIIs.

His sister Marion, also known as 'Penny', (Mom told me she got this nick-name because she was so cheap) waitressed at a restaurant. Marion was a strange character. She would take home the bread leftovers from people's plates and from the bread baskets that went back to the kitchen. But, it didn't stop there; she would scrape the left-over meat from customers' plates and put it into a brown paper bag. She would save this bagged food for another meal or feed the leavings to her mother. I wonder if anyone got sick from these acts. She offered it to us kids, but we snubbed our noses at it. For a while, Mom had a part time job at the same place as a waitress and when a customer came in and sat down at a table, mom waited on them. Marion would spy this event and put a glass of water on the table and expect mom to split her tips with her. What a cheapskate!

Numerous unforgivable deeds seemed commonplace between my grandparents. A story I heard third hand: Grandfather had a gambling problem and lost a good sum of their savings. He was never forgiven for these deeds and was scorned until his death. He spent his life alone, although he did amuse us kids with funny faces and jokes and would take us to down cellar to see his workshop and treasures. He made his own food, usually chicken soup, and he and his wife never again slept in the same bed together.

Grandma never had meaningful conversations with us kids or with my mother. I always thought that from the side, she looked like George Washington on the dollar bill because of the way she set her gray hair and the shape of her face and her closed lips. She was a big woman and her short legs were huge and reminded me of elephant's legs and feet. I remember my grandmother cleaning homes and businesses on her hands and knees well into her late 70s. I don't know how she did it!

So as you can imagine, I was told a thousand times: don't play with fire, don't waste your food, use your head to think instead of for a hat rack, put things back where you got them from…To this day, I can still hear my father's voice in my head saying these things to us boys.

My father was in WWII in Germany and was shot twice, once in the leg and once in the head. He went through several episodes of traumatic stress and it affected his whole life and ours. I recall only one war story that I heard from my mother. She said, "When your father was fighting the war against the Germans, he was wounded and laid on the ground motionless covered by other dead soldiers. The German soldiers came around and checked his fallen comrade and him, but Dad was smart enough to play dead. He was wounded but never made a sound or a movement as not to give him away that he was still alive. The Germans soldiers never discovered his condition!" That must have been very tense for him and haunted him for years.

My father was not a patient man and not well educated. Dad just barely made it through 8th grade and never applied his education until he married our mother. My older brother, Aiden, was born while my father was in the service, so he lacked that fatherly bond from the start which created resentment in the house, which affected my brother's life and ours. I recently saw a black and white photo of Dad in his army uniform knelling down with one arm around Aiden. You could tell they were strangers. I feel they never had a loving bond together. The lack of a bond affected my brother's life, and he eventually moved out when he was 18 years old because of this friction.

I recently found out that when Dad was on his leave from the service, he would live at his mother's house because he was not married to our mother but to another woman in South Carolina where he had done his basic training. He also had a daughter with this woman. He finally received a divorce and married our mother a few months before I was born. The day my father died, Mom told us boys that we had a sister in South Carolina and all these years, Mom had been sending child support to his daughter until she was 18 years old. What a trooper my mother was. I have met Dad's daughter Barb and her family and stayed with them in Washington and she has met my family too. It was good to have some completion for all of us, and we still keep in touch.

My father was always fighting, breaking and smashing things around the house, and taking everything out mostly on our mother. As kids and allies of our mother, this hurt us a lot. I can vividly remember one time when we younger boys were woken up with his hysteria and yelling. While in our pajamas, we quietly snuck into the bedroom above the kitchen where there was a floor vent which we could look through and be witness to all this terror.

Looking down through the vent's opening, we heard their enraged words. Frightened by this bad energy and fighting, Dad would threaten mom, hit her, and smash articles she owned or cherished. We cried during the whole altercation! Scared and frightened, we yelled down the vent, crying with rage and fear: "Stop hitting our mother!" We were both shaking and disturbed. I can still see this image in my mind and will someday paint it as a picture to release this bad energy. Dad finally mellowed out some because our mom had a secret weapon! She threatened him with the fact that if he killed her, he would have to take care of his sons!

As a young boy, I can recall sitting at the dinner table and forgetting how to hold my silverware and in which hand. Dad couldn't understand why I was acting this way but I was sincere. He instructed me to sit under the table while they ate and not to come until I knew how to hold my utensils. During this episode, I remember my brothers and father kicking me and sometimes it hurt. I finally was able to come up from the floor but not until everyone else was through with their dinner.

My younger brother, David, always sided with my father. I guess so he wouldn't get punished as much as I did. As the middle of three children, I ended up getting beat up by my two brothers and my father. These episodes made me swear to me that, "I would NEVER be like this—NEVER!!"

Growing up, I was no angel, but, I did deserve some punishments and I got the belt a lot. Dad would have us bend over the tub while he struck us on our butt. Mom would use the yardstick that she kept behind the bathroom door. At times, she would keep us in line by just banging the yardstick against the wall.

My mother pushed my father to find a steady job where he could make a respectable living using his body instead of his mind. He became a professional house painter where he stayed for 15 years. His first specialty was painting church steeples, then, houses and interiors. When we boys moved out of the house, married, and had our own homes, Dad helped us boys with the painting and wallpapering.

As a boy, I learned from watching, asking questions, although not always getting an answer, and doing menial tasks for him on his paying jobs. He would say, "More hands make easier and faster results." He was a fast painter and made good money. Many times my father would see an advertisement in the newspaper for painter wanted, or knew someone who had a cottage. He would offer to paint inside or outside in exchange for free rent during our stay. We were lucky to have this advantage!

As kids, my brothers and I would help him on some of his painting jobs, usually by scraping, priming, and cleaning up. When we did paint the finish coat, I remember his favorite saying: "Slop it on, and smooth it out!" "Even today when I paint, I hear his voice in my head saying, "Slop it on, and smooth it out..." When I taught painting to my kids and friends I always used this phrase. Sometimes, I'd catch myself having internal conversations with my father in the form of approval questions, and I acknowledge the trades he passed on to me as a "Thank you Dad!"

Following his painting career, he studied to advance his profession by taking a civil service exam to become a custodian in the public school system. I remember Mom helping him learn the questions and answers to the pre-test. He retired after 25 years and worked in three different schools. He was somewhat handy around the house and would try fixing things. Sometimes he would, and sometimes they remained broken. I can remember other times when he would get very frustrated or things would not be working out for him and he would say, "God Dam it!" and uncontrollably destroy what he was working on!

I know that he had a limited knowledge of car repairs because he would buy a used car and trade it in every two years instead of repairing them. He was funny too; when he bought another car, if there was a sound or a squeak of any magnitude, he would take it back to the dealer until it was fixed. If it wasn't fixed after several tries, he would curse the dealer and say, "I'm never going to buy another car from him!" "If he thinks I will, he can "eat a yard-of-my shit!" His teachings and observations were passed on, or incorporated into our beings, and informed our experiences, legacies, and interactions with others. I'm glad I remember these times but I never have gone to this point of anger like he did...

As I look back on my childhood, I did things which affected his attitude toward me. In his youth, my father made a scale model of an airplane out of wood which must have taken him many hours to complete. Well, we kids played with his plane down in the cellar. One time, I had the great idea to cut a hole in the top so I could get inside to be its pilot. What a stupid hateful person I was. I only realize this because I am now a father and grandfather myself and can put it into his perspective!

Another thing I did was Dad brought back trinkets from the war. One item was a pair of wooden shoes from Holland. Here I go with another brilliant idea: I drilled two holes in their sides so I could put a string inside to tie them to my feet to keep them on. I basically ruined them! "I'm sorry Dad for these things I did and ask your forgiveness..." Well, life goes on. I wonder what else I will remember. I'm reflecting on this now because I can also think of a few things my kids did to disappoint me.

As years went on, Dad mellowed out toward his end where he could enjoy his grandchildren. Eventually, his smoking caught up with him, and he ended up in the hospital. One time in the veteran's hospital, he had his arteries replaced from his aorta to both of his legs, and another time, when he couldn't breathe, they installed a pacemaker. Being a good son, when he got home from the hospital, I rigged up a signal buzzer from his couch bed downstairs to my mother's bedroom upstairs, and showed him how to use it in case he needed help from Mom. It lasted about a week and worked fine, but eventually, he died at 67 years old taking his last breathe lying on our couch. That was the end of an era, 36 years ago...

GRANDPA AND GRAMMY

Funny how things tweak your memory and you recall a place or a special person in your life. We all do it. I just like to write about it. Being a grandfather myself, I often think of my grandfather, Sandy, Papa, my mother's father, a lot these days.

I was named Sandy after him. History stated that the first male grandchild to be named Sandy in the family would receive my grandfather's silver baby cup from 1897. This was very significant for his family because he was the first male to be born in three generations! When my daughter had a son, she gave him the middle name Sandy, so I presented the silver baby cup over to him in 2009 passing on the legacy. Well off to the story!

We visited Maine often as a family. In the old days it took about 8 hours to get from our home in Massachusetts, to Belfast, Maine via back roads. Now it takes four and a half hours because of super highways!

This is how a typical trip to Maine was: "I have to go the bathroom!" I said. Mom said, "I'm hungry too Honey, let's stop and have lunch." Dad remarked, "I'll pull over at the next church or cemetery so we can have lunch.", "I'm getting hungry also and would like a cigarette." Dad said, "Hey, there's a cemetery over there!" With a quick turn of the wheel of our yellow, 1960 Chevy station wagon, he pulled into the little dirt road, and parked near a trash barrel full of old plant stuff, and a water spigot where we could wash up after lunch. "This is great!" said Mom. We all got out and Dad swung the tailgate down to use for a work area and seat. David and I went off to explore the grave stones to see what treasures we could find. In the mean time, Mom made our lunch while Dad had his smoke.

Mom took out the old red metal Coca-Cola cooler and began assembling our lunch. She took out a loaf of white bread, two glass bowls, and some utensils. One bowl had potato salad in it that she made last night and the other was empty. She opened up a can of corned-beef, you know, that's the one with the little key on the side that usually broke, and emptied it into the empty bowl. She added mayonnaise and mustard to it and mixed it up to a creamy consistency so she could spread it on the bread. She made five sandwiches, 1 ½ each for me and Dad, and one each for my brother and mother. Mom knew that Dad and I always had hollow legs that had to be filled. She poured four glasses of red Kool-Aid and on the ground she spread out and an old, khaki-colored Army blanket for us kids off to the side of the car as not to block their view.

While all the lunch prep was going on, David and I went exploring the cemetery. "Hey, this one is older than that one," said David. "No, mine is older by six months, and has an angel with wings and bones on it!" I exclaimed. We looked for people who were born on our birthdays, odd and scary pictures, and people who only lived a few days. At that age, everything was interesting and spiked our curiosities. Off in the distance we heard, "Kids, lunch is ready!" We raced back to the car. I usually beat my brother because my long, skinny legs could move faster than his short, chubby legs.

Mom had everything set up just right on the blanket for us boys, and they sat on the ends of the tailgate with their food between them. I said to David while lapping my lips with my food covered tongue, "Boy, there's nothing in this world that can compare to a corned-beef sandwich and potato salad!" David agreed by moaning with his mouth filled. Then David spilled his drink and made a fuss over it, while I couldn't be concerned because I was consumed with gulping up my lunch as fast as I could. Mom took out an apple and cut it up for us boys to have for dessert. We boys ate like it was our last meal except, I always left my crust on my plate. I never liked my crust! Eventually, it began to sprinkle a little, and Mom said, "Boys, gather up your things and get in the car so you will be comfortable for the rest of the trip." We got in, Mom packed up the lunch fixings, and Dad had another cigarette.

It didn't take long for David and me to fall asleep from our great picnic lunch and the motion of the moving car. Dad always drove and Mom navigated. At times during our nap, I would be half woken up by their bickering about directions or the smell of Dad's cigarette. Before we knew it, Mom would say excitedly, "Wake up boys, were at the cottage!"

My father would have a two-week vacation, and we would spend it at Papa's cottage on Swan Lake. There was a row boat, a small motor, I think an 11/2 hp Johnson, and a canoe to use. My father would take us out in the motor boat sometimes. I remember watching how he starting the outboard motor. First he turned the gas on, then, primed the float until some fuel came out the top, and he set the throttle to start. Next he manually wound the knotted rope around the flywheel. It took a few pulls to get it started, but it beat rowing. As I got older, Dad let us boys take it out by ourselves just as long as we stayed in sight of the cottage.

However, the first time dad showed me how to run the boat and motor, I remember him teaching me how to steer the boat into the dock, he said, "Give it some gas." So I did, but, well..., not accustomed to the throttle sensitivity, I gunned it by mistake and ended going around in a circle and almost hitting the rocks and tipping the gunnels of the boat within two inches of our side-swiping wave. Well, with practice, I got to be a 'pro'.

My brother and I loved to fish and swim. We would spend hours off the shore or on the rocks fishing for the 'Big One'. When David told this story, he would always hold up his hands to show me how big the 'Big One' was. We mostly caught kivers, perch, and sunfish, but it was fun. My grandfather would show us how to dress the fish and fry it up in a pan of butter, salt, and pepper. It was great after getting through all those little bones, but the best part was, we caught them.

My grandfather caught many large fish in his life, and I remember one prized trout he caught. In his kitchen, over the top of the outside entrance door, he drew a picture with a pencil tracing around the outside of the actual trout's body and colored in the details with crayons. It was there for at least 30 years.

One time, my brother, David, and I were casting for fish in the cove near the cottage. I had a special new lure on the end of my line that looked like a fish with three hooks on one end. Well, I casted the pole in the air and the line on its upward arch of the lure, caught my brother's cheek with one of its hooks. He cried and made me leave it in his cheek so he could get emergency help from Mom to take it out. He was OK and a bandage and a kiss were in order.

When David was five and I was eight, we decided to go fishing early in the day. For a long time, we followed the large boulders that lined the shore to a small cove. This cove had a fresh water spring that emptied into it, and it was also our drinking water source. We fished for a while and my younger brother got bored, so he left. I continued to fish. After a while I got a bite. It tugged and played with my line back and forth and headed under the large protruding boulders. David hearing me yelling to the line, came back to see what I was doing and finally, after a fierce tough, I was able to free the fish from under the rocks and reeled it in. Just as it broke the waterline, we were both shocked! A 2-foot long, slimy, green eel came up out of the water and wrapped itself around my fishing line and right up my pole! 'Scared' was not the word for an 8-year-old boy! Quickly taking it out of the water, I ran out to the lawn area and threw the pole, eel and all onto a grassy knoll and I watched it wiggled for a while before it was exhausted and succumbed. I couldn't wait to show my grandfather what I caught!

My grandfather came up that evening and he showed me how to dress it. First he made a cut down its whole body to the tail and gutted its insides. Then he cut it up into 6-inch pieces. He added salt, pepper, and then he placed the pieces in a pot of boiling water for a while. Next, he took the bones out and then put it in a frying pan with butter and salt. He called this cast iron frying pan a 'Spiders'. I guess this is a Maine name! It was surprisingly delicious. It was great just like he said. I always liked fish.

My grandfather and grandmother Rose would come up for supper many times during the week. It was always a treat. My grandmother loved to bake and would make some donuts or donut holes and bring them for dessert or breakfast the next day. Us kids would put some sugar in a paper bag and shake the donuts around in the bag to have sugar-covered donuts. Boy, what a treat. Grandmothers love to spoil their grandchildren, as I know!

My grandfather, and his friend Carl Webber along with his sons, built the cottage in 1949. The cottage was made up of two floors. Downstairs was an electric stove, a sink with water pumped out of the lake to wash dishes, a refrigerator, a writing desk where we kids could draw or color, a table with 4 chairs, two rocking chairs, two couches, and a wood stove for those cold summer nights, and a black and white TV with rabbitears that received two channels. Upstairs were the sleeping quarters. Partway up the set of wooden stairs to upstairs was a large wood door, fixed horizontally between the floors. It was operated by a rope and pulley system using old window weights for counter balance. This was used to keep the wood stove heat downstairs for a while, and then we opened it up at bedtime to heat the bedroom. The bedroom was just one large, long room with no partitions and a row of casement windows overlooking the lake. There were 4 beds, two double beds with high ornate carved head boards made by my great-grandfather, and a couple of single cots. There were two bureaus filled with spare bedding. At the end of the room between the beds was an old 1934 Philco AM floor model radio, which hummed when you first turned it on, but after it warmed up, it would work fine.

My brother and I went swimming every day at the cottage. As I recall, Mom would wade in enough to get her legs wet and pat water on the rest of her body. She really didn't like fresh water swimming because she was brought up swimming in the ocean at the foot of their road. Now Dad, he would start back on the shore and then run into the lake with a quick action of his arms going over his head and dive into the surface of the water. As he surfaced from below, he'd spit out some water while briskly shaking water from his hair.

Now Grandpa Sandy; I think I only saw my grandfather get wet in the lake once up to his rolled up pants legs and long underwear. Now that I think back, I can remember my grandfather wearing his long underwear all year round along with his flannel shirt and suspenders holding his gray flannel pants up. In the summer time, he would roll up his shirt sleeves, and in cold weather, he would wear them down and buttoned. He must have liked his heat or was it that he disliked cold! I'm not sure.

At his house in Belfast, he would have a fire going in the kitchen cook stove even in the summer. He would cut his dry wood very small so he could have a very hot fire to get the metal heated. Most of the time he would be sitting in his rocking chair one foot away from the stove, while on his left side was a Kelvinator refrigerator and a bookcase. He would sit there most of the day studying his horse-racing books which kept him occupied for years. He would always put his left foot about waist high on the side of the Kelvinator refrigerator and used it to rock his rocker while he studied. Well, over time, 25-30 years, the refrigerator's white enamel paint was right down to the bare metal in the shape of a two foot elongated foot print! He often relaxed by sipping a mixture of warm water, sugar, and P.M. Whiskey. He always had a pipe in his mouth filled with Prince Albert tobacco in a can which he lit by taking a wooden safety match from his flannel shirt pocket and touching its end to the side of the hot wood stove. One time, he saved about 20 of these tobacco cans for me so I could organize my small electronic parts in them. Well, to tell you the truth, I really didn't use these parts after all so the parts sat in the cans unused for years. About 5 years ago I emptied the cans and sent Papa's tobacco cans to each of my first cousins, aunts, uncles, and my brothers, so they could have a piece of Papa with them forever.

My grandfather owned a clothing store on Main Street in Belfast, Maine, Stephen and Son. His mother ran the store when he was younger and he took it over later on. He had work clothes by Carter, long underwear, socks, hunting outfits, tee shirts, flannel shirts, etc. He did a good business. I remember his store was always busy with his friends, and they'd sit by the wood stove and talk about life, hunting, and horse racing. He always had a visitor in there with whom to chat. I guess he was building up a clientele. The building housed two businesses; his and another business. There was a small connecting door off their joining stock rooms which they kept open to share stories and for comfort. The other store was Howard Cratch's Confectionery didn't care, it made us feel special. In the later years, after my grandfather closed the store, he continued doing deliveries for Howard out of his car's seat and trunk.

Sometimes he would take me with him, and tell me stories about the places we were going to and the people we were going to meet. Once or twice he took me to Isleboro Island off the coast of Belfast, where we had to take a ferry out of Lincolnville to cross the bay. This island was seven miles long and one mile wide and we would cover every store, delivering or taking orders. That was a great time. Sometimes we would get a quick bite to eat, but most of the time, my grandma would pack a lunch of homemade biscuits with a piece of ham inside and some delicious homemade dessert or a piece of fruit. He would have his thermos of instant coffee, mixed with milk and sugar and I might have a glass jar of some fruit juice.

When I was 14 years old he took me for a ride on the back roads of Searsport Maine to show off his new, yellow, 1964 Chevy with the big engine and the passing gear. He liked to show off for us kids. One time, he shocked me when he pulled over to the side of the road and asked me, "Would you like to drive my new car?" Without hesitation I said, "Wouldn't I!" I swapped places with him and he showed me how everything worked. In those days, people didn't wear seat belts. No problem! I moved up the seat so I could touch the pedals and he instructed me what to do and how to work everything. After a few abrupt starts, I finally was driving on the road, about 20 mph I guess. I got going and he said, "Give it a little more gas to feel the power it has." While being a little cautious and scared, I did, but I followed his prompts. I was going about 50 mph now! Suddenly, as I was going up a hill, he said, "Hold the steering wheel tight with your two hands, now press the gas pedal to the floor and hold it down, and I did!" Well, the passing gear kicked in, shocking the 'SHIT!' out of me! It pinned my head back in the seat and I started to sweat some. I remember hitting 80 or 90 mph! After a spell, he told me to pull over to the side of the road. With his excited, lit-up face; he asked me, "How did I like the feel of the car and its power?" I was fit for no words for a few seconds! "It was fab-u-lous!" I said, while wiping the sweat off my brow and smiling from end to end. We never told Grandma but my mother knew. A few years later, when my younger brother David was 14, he took him out and they shared the same experiences together.

Another thing I learned from Grandpa was how to shave. In his bathroom was a big mirror over the sink with two incandescent bulbs with pull chains, one on each side. I stood back and watched Grandpa get ready to shave. First, I remember watching him put the shaving cream on his face after he mixed it up in a cup with a brush. Then he took his razor blade and made what looked like he was making 'lines' on his face with the razor removing the shaving cream. When he was finished, he let me touch his face to feel his smooth, shaved section or the remaining whiskers. Then he would rinse out his razor. The last thing he did was take some water in his cupped hands, and splash it all over his face while making a noise like, "Burr!" then he would walk out of the bathroom and on the left was the door to the cellar. On this door was a contraption he made that had a roller on the top held up with two wood brackets and on the roller was a continuous cloth towel that was sewn together by

Grandma. This was 'His' towel and only "His" towel. He was always scared of germs!

After a few episodes of watching him shave, I finally asked him to teach me how to shave. I must have been 13 or so. He began first by taking out his real razor blade by twisting its handle. The top magically opened up like a butterfly exposing the razor blade. In place of his razor blade he put inside the razorblades' original piece of cardboard that was around this sharp steel blade and I use this cardboard for my razor blade. He mixed up the lather and let me put it on my face. He showed me how to draw those lines and what direction or passes to make over my face. While looking in the mirror, I made all kinds of facial movements with my face to clean all the cream off my face. Eventually, my face was absent of shaving cream. I finished, and washed my face by making the "Burr!" sound and used a towel in the bathroom to dry my face. I went into Grandpa, sitting in his rocking chair, and let him feel my smooth face! He chuckled and said, "What a good job!"

It's great to have a grandfather with whom to share man things with, and a grandmother to show you how to bake, cook, play the piano, sing, and tell us boy's bible stories. I hope to share these things with my grandson Sandy as I did now with you. Time to show him how to shave!!

I guess I'm old fashion, but I respected my grandparents. I learned so much from them and, unlike a parent when you can't do anything right, grand parents don't pick on you about the little things. It's their duty and privilege to pass on their interests and knowledge of how times were in their days so they can put today's happenings into perspective.

MY BROTHER AIDEN

Being the middle boy of three I got it from both sides. My brother Aiden was seven year older than me, and David was three years younger but 35 pounds heavier. Aiden was born the same day as my uncle Nick was tragically killed. That day was 11/11, and I often wonder if that date was significant and how it played out in our lives. Some day it will come to me!

AIDEN grew up in Belfast Maine until the age of six and then we moved with our parents to Marlborough Massachusetts. The apartment was convenient to my grandparent's home in Marlborough. AIDEN was in HedriCK School for a while, then we moved to Francisco Street when I was three years old but what I know is from hear say and old photos.

Something funny I noticed about AIDEN was his walking habit. He would always walk on his tip-toes. It was funny to see this but now I know where this came from. My Grandfather did the same thing. I wonder if it was a hereditary trait passed on to certain descendents. It wasn't passed onto me!

When AIDEN was in high school, an art teacher, Mr. Sears, took a fondness of AIDEN and taught him how to draw and paint art. In fact, I have one of his first oil paintings hanging in my house. After high school, he went to a college of art in Boston for his BS in art and eventually finished at the University of Nantucket where he received his Master's in Art. Being a colorful guy, while living in Boston Arthur when went to a Halloween party at a friend's place and decide to be a Leprechaun. He put green food coloring and in the tub and dyed his whole body green, hair and all. Talk about colorful! He was the hit of the party. After college, he taught art in many schools and establishments over the years. Recently, he is rubbing elbows next to the Andy Withcome and other famous artist in Rockport Maine with his new art show.

As a young boy, seven years younger, I didn't end up chumming around with him and his friends. Most friends would just stop by for five minutes and he would go off with them.

We all went to his high school graduation the whole family in tow, grandparents and all. He took me along to junk yards to get parts for his jalopies. This was always lots of fun. He was on the freshman football team in high school, but his career was cut short by a broken leg during a game. He built a dog sled for Scouts and drew all the time. I always made a point to visit him every time he moved as well as helping him move from place to place. I believe I was a good brother to him!

One time, in 1966 when I was 16 years old, I decided to visit Aiden in New York City. I had never gone on an adventure like this in my life! I bummed a ride to Newington Connecticut from a fellow ham radio operator of mine, who took me to an event at ARRL museum, for an open house event. He then took me to the Hartford bus station and I was on my way.

I had never been on a long bus ride like this by myself. I found a window seat and got comfortable for the long ride. I took out my maps and studied them for a few minutes. The bus started to fill up and there were only three spots left. An older man sat next to me and introduced himself as Larry and said he lived in New York City. Larry seemed to be interested in what I said and he asked me, "What part of the city are you going to?" I told him, "Greenwich Village." I continued to look out the window and became a little sleepy. Every time we approached an interesting site in the city, he leaned over and put his left hand on my right knee and pointed to the site with his right hand. At the time, I didn't think anything about it, but after a while and many points of interest, it felt kinda strange. He said to me, "We still have an hour to go and you should get some sleep because the city is big and you will have to walk a lot." It sounded like good advice to me, so I shut my eyes tighter and drifted off deeply for a while. I woke up when the bus stopped as we arrived at the bus station in NYC. I gathered up my belongings and started walking out in the line. As we got to the ground, he turned around and shook my hand and he handed me a piece of paper with his address and phone number and told me, "If you get lost or lonely you can always stop by my place." So I put the note in my pocket. I never gave it another thought. I got myself orientated with my map and by asking some questions, and I was on my quest to my brother's place. Aiden lived in lower Greenwich Village where he had a cooking/bouncer job in a bar called Standees'.

I walked for hours and finally came to Washington Square. I found his apartment but he was not there. I set off to find him at his work. After walking around in what seemed circles, I finally found the place. It was a small, dark restaurant/bar in the basement of a building. When I walked in, he was making soup. Now, Aiden was never an expert on cooking but he had an idea what goes into soup from hanging around with Grandfather. He said, "I get off of work in an hour and a half so here is my key to the apartment." I found it after circling around for a while and I dropped off my bag. I then walked around until he got out of work getting my bearings by noting how many lefts and rights I took and landmarks and street signs.

The next day Aiden had to work but he fixed me up with his friend. Her name was Rickie. She was about 25-26 years old, cute and a little over weight. She knew her way around the city and was my tour guide. She wanted to know what I wanted to see and I told her I wanted to go to the night club, 'Electric Center'. I had heard about it but never seen the inside. She cleared it with Aiden and came over and picked me up and we walked to it. Inside, it was huge with lots of moving, colorful lights and large speakers with dancers on multi-levels throughout the building. They also had projected images on the walls. This was quite a display for a small town boy! We danced and walked around inside. My eyes were popping out of my head and my ears were full of sounds I'd never heard before. They sounded like an orchestra then they switched to electronic music. I'm not sure how long we were there but it was getting late so she walked me back to Aiden's.

I was still tired from my trip down. On the way to Aiden's place, we came along four colored men heading toward us. They stopped us and asked, "What do you think of the United Nations?" I can't remember what my answer was but it freaked me out to say the least. I was never exposed to this type of experience coming from an old New England town that was predominantly white and secluded. The next day Aiden asked me how the date went. I told him and he also clued me in that area was one of the biggest coke sections in lower Manhattan. I didn't even know what 'coke' was...other than the drink!

Another time Aiden was going to school and student teaching at the University of Art. I contacted him and found out his wife Helen was pregnant and due to have a baby soon. So I got my ducks in order, made excuses for my sudden trip, and got in my car the next day after I received a call from my brother of his son's birth. They named him Adam because he was their first child. I finally made it in about five hours and managed to take photos with my Polaroid instant camera so I could secretly show my mother her first grandson. Another time, I travelled to Amherst with my brother Cedric because Aiden had a car for me to take home. It was a 1946 Buick. At the time I had a 1964 Ford Mustang Ford convertible with a small 6 cylinder engine and had rented a tow bar to tow the Buick home. We got it all hooked up and ready to move off and... the Mustang didn't have enough power to move this BIG car. The clutch and brakes were overheating and due to overheating and burning and I didn't want to hurt our car, so we abandoned this venture.

In 1975, Aiden got a job as an art teacher in North Dakota as an art teacher in 1975. North Dakota is about 2000 miles away from New England. I had just gotten married to my first wife and we decided that this would make a great honeymoon road trip across the states and back through the middle of the country. This gave us time to be alone and explore ourselves as a married couple. We stayed a while and we got to know Aiden's son Adam better. He was playing with all the Indian children in the neighborhood. I had a small camper on the back of our truck which made traveling more bearable. Being on our honeymoon, when we got the 'Urge,' and we did a lot of times on the road, I'd just pull over and perform the act! On the way back we stopped in Culver City and visited a cave as well as junk stores. One store had a shirt of four presidents kneeling down from the back showing their asses with a saying: "Scene from the back of Mt. Rushmore'." It was too funny! For a wedding present, Aiden gave us a pick of one of six of his large original oil paintings. I have it hanging in my living room. Over the years, I made numerous trips to other places Aiden lived, such as: Washington DC, Virginia, Maryland, South Carolina, and finally, Eastport, Maine. I believe that Eastport was his last move and the best place he has ever lived where he can express his artistic qualities and have many friends and supporters. I've moved him many times and drove thousands of miles and all for what? I needed to connect and get to know my brother. As you remember, he left home around 18 years old and never came back to visit. I needed him in my life. My mother always found a way to keep in touch with him and let me know what was going on with him. She always encouraged and supported me in my visits so she could have some communication with him and his family. He was a good friend and brother to me those days.

I visited him in Eastport many, many times over the years. Twice my new wife Lavinia and I went up to put on a dance program in the community building for the residents of Eastport. We had a great turnout and taught all the dances. Whenever we visit, we run into someone who was at the dance and they want to know when we were going to run another one. Another time I rebuilt the electric system in his house and boxed it all in so it would look more presentable. I feel appreciated that I can lend my talents to help him make his life better.

Aiden was not a well man. A smoker like our father since he was 15 years old, his habit finally caught up with him. And at age 55, he suffered with a twisted and blocked bowel which resulted in its removal and was corrected with a bag taped to his side to collect his feces. My grandfathers both had the same problem.

In 2015, Aiden's conditions got worsened. He was in and out of several hospitals and nursing home and could not take care of himself. We visited him twice in the health care facilities. His conditions were worsening and I felt that his time was fading away. I always love and admired my brother. I felt bad that he had no quality life as a kid home life in Marlboro. After my last trip, His son called and notified me that he passed peacefully in his bed at his home on December 16, 2016. He was 72 years old. As I said earlier, Mom is in a nursing home now at the age of 92 ½ and my younger brother and I decided to shield her from the truth of his passing. We didn't know how it would affect her. Well two weeks later, Mom floored me by saying, "I guess Aiden is no longer with us…" I never told her and the nursing staff didn't either. She must have heard him talking to her through the heavenly conduit and their blood connection. She never talked about it again.

It's June now and the other day Mom asked me who was still alive in her family. I told her that her brother Tim and sister Rosetta were still alive. Then she asked me how Aiden was doing and I said, "He's fine Mom."

MY BROTHER AIDEN

When I was born in 1950, we lived on Chessville Street in the French section of Marlboro. My older brother Aiden went to Mitchville School across the road. Mom became pregnant gain in

July of 1952 it became obvious that our small apartment wouldn't be adequate for the five of us.

Mom, wanted to buy a house, and investigated Dad's government benefits for his bad ear and wounds. She managed to get a 10% disability for his injury and they were awarded $1,000 in benefits. Mom used this money for a potential 10% down payment on a house. My parents found a house at 68 Franklyn Street for $7,000, exactly right across the street from where my father grew up as a young boy. Aiden was born in March at a Boston area hospital. Mom said to the doctor, "There must be a mistake. He can't be my baby, because he's nine pounds and has dark hair". My older brother and I had blond hair and much smaller frames. As I understand it, Aiden was actually a twin because after the doctor delivered him, she felt something else in her stomach. It was a little girl, but she was a still-born.

Franklin Street was closer to Main Street, and like Chestnut Street, had a school at the end of the road with a playground and a corner variety store for food, cigarettes and candy. It was a grand old house. Outside, it had two big pine trees on one side, hedges in front, a dirt driveway, and a small 'L' shaped backyard. Behind the house was a small dead end street, Mica Street, with four houses on it and a hill. The house itself had a cellar and a first and second floor. On the front was a wrap-around porch with ladder type lattice from the railings to the porch roof. Over the front door it said in script, "68 Franklin Street"; it's funny that the past owner of the house was John Franklin. Franklin Street was originally School Street but when John Franklin's brother died in the war, they changed the name to Franklin Street.

On the first floor was an old country kitchen with huge black cast-iron kerosene cooking stove, a white, self-standing sink, with storage cabinets underneath, a refrigerator, and two windows and five doors. Off the kitchen were two small rooms. The first room we used as a pantry and the other was a bathroom with a deep iron clawed foot white tub, a sink and a toilet. Off the kitchen, next to the stove, was a dining room with a built in corner china closet. Off this room was the living room. It had sliding pocket doors and three windows and a side door which went into the hallway to the front door and the stair to the second level.

Upstairs, there were three bedrooms off the hallway, each with a closet. All the rooms had ornate pull chain ceiling lights. Mom and Dad had the big bedroom and David and I had the front bedroom and our older brother Aiden had the side room to himself. My bed was near the double window and David's crib was across from me against the wall. There was a walk-in room storage attic that connected with our parent's bedroom. Dad wallpapered our bedroom with 'The Lone Ranger and Tonto' wallpaper. How many times we both dreamt about "Hi-ho Silver, away" and his adventures. It was perfect for two boys!

One of my first memories of David was of him sitting in his crib and banging his head on the railing repeatedly. I guess it was either a calming motion or an attention getter. As he got bigger he was able to bump his head and move the crib right across the room and up to the side of my bed. Eventually David developed a callus on his forehead! David couldn't say my name so his nickname for me was "ToTo." I'm not sure how he came up with this label, as it doesn't resemble my name. As we got older, David and I got twin beds. Mine was still next to the window.

Being three years older than David, eventually the room became too small for the two of us. Aiden moved out to go to college and I moved into his bedroom, so David had our bedroom all to himself. As we got older this room was a great place to escape from when we were sent to our rooms for doing something bad. Remember those lattices' ladders on the front porch? When we got older and were sent to our bedroom as a punishment, we used them as escape ladders so we could play and get back into the house without being caught. One of us would tell the other if the coast was clear.

Downstairs, the pantry was a fun place to play. On one side was a series of coat hooks arranged halfway up the wall with wainscot on the bottom and plaster on top. The hooks were loaded with coats and hats and across from them was a tall, white, metal storage cabinet with canned goods and food packages, and a window. Mom always hung her purse on these hooks making this the perfect hiding place for us to sneak into her purse and take out change to spend at our corner store, Billie's. Today I know why we had so many cavities: Blame it on Billie's! Mom always knew we snuck into her purse to find loose change but never let on. She would just throw her change into her purse for this purpose. Mom's purse, along with her folding money, always had that 'mom' smell, kind of sweet and perfumed. In those days, our parents would send us down to the corner store to pick up a quart of whole milk, a loaf of white Wonder Bread and cigarettes, each costing about 25 cents or less. There would always be a little left over for a service charge; CANDY!

One time, David was playing in the pantry and was very quiet. Mom might have been outdoors hanging clothes and when she came back into the house, she found David quietly sitting on the pantry floor removing all the labels from the canned goods that were stored in the white cabinet. When it came time to make dinner, she didn't know if she was opening string beans or dog food!

We got a German shepherd dog and we named her "Holly" because she was Mom's gift for Christmas. She was a good, smart dog and loved following us kids around the neighborhood. One Christmas or Thanksgiving, David and Holly went for a hike around the neighborhoods and came back with a fully cooked turkey. Mom looked out the kitchen window and there was David and the dog both sitting in the snow eating the turkey. We never found out whose it was. I felt bad for the family who didn't have their dinner that day.

Another time, after a big snow storm, we took a walk up Middle Street and decided to jump across a stone wall onto the roof of a neighbor's garage. There was a separation of about 18 inches from the roof and the 12-foot high retaining wall. We made it to the flat, snow-covered roof where David coaxed me to jump off into the snow, about a distance of about 12 feet to the ground. The snow was very deep compared to my little body. I jumped, and got stuck into the snow up to my waist. I tried to get loose but I could not budge. My boots were stuck deep in the snow. I eventually wiggled out of my buried snow boots and had to walk home in my stocking feet. Dad was not a happy camper. He sent my older brother back to recover my boots and I was sent to my room.

One time I climbed nearly to the top of one of the tall pine trees next to our club house and decided to cut the top off for a Christmas tree. I tied Dad's hand saw to my belt loop and positioned myself at the perfect place to make a great looking Christmas tree. I began to cut and half the way through the limb, the saw got stuck. I called David to help me but he wasn't very good at climbing trees. All of these efforts might have been better if it was nearer Christmas instead of the summer so we could have used the top section for our Christmas tree! When my father drove home from work, he immediately noticed that the tree top was hanging down. I got the devil again. David said, "Sandy did it, I told him not to, but he did it anyway." I always got punished but David sided with my father and usually escaped the punishment. Eventually Dad cut the two trees down to add more light to that side of the house and Mom could look out that window to see us walk home from school or from Bacon's store.

As boys, we would sneak into vacant houses and pretend they were haunted to plague David so he would run home or cry. We also snuck into the cellar of old man Stephen's rag and metal warehouse and played cops and robbers. We would wait until a Sunday when it wasn't open and climb the fence that was blocking a steep hill. In the cellar we would sneak into a broken windows and search for buried treasure. I can remember all the nightmares we had about falling into holes and meeting 'boogie men'. David used to get scared easily and had to hold our clothes as we led the way.

Mom would drive us kids to the town dump, leave us off for an hour or so while she did her food shopping, and come back to pick us up. We always found tons of treasures to cart home and put them in the cellar or club house. We never worried about getting hurt or abducted in those days.

As we got older, we started working on cars and having our own. Aiden would take us to the auto junkyard so he could get parts for his jalopies and we could explore the other treasures. David and I together bought a white1964, Ford Mustang convertible with a four speed non-syncro transmission from a man on French Hill. It was so cool. Over the years, David had a Firebird, Datsun 240Z, A-M-C Pacer, a 1974 Corvette, just to name a few of his cars. We shared a '53 Mercury for a while too. We both worked in the same grocery store 'Wonderful Market' at different times. He at stocking shelves and me worked as a cashier.

I went to college for my second year to study electronics and David went to college to study bookkeeping and accounting. We had a few double dates with girls we met at an amusement park and both of us played the trumpet in the high school band. We eventually went our own ways, moving, college, marriage and kids but always staying friends and doing things together that we enjoyed. My little brother is 63 years old now. This year, he decided to come to one of the class reunions with me, a first time for him. I've gone to every one of my reunions. Maybe he will go this summer again with me.

CHAPTER 2

CHILDHOOD ADVENTURES

BIRTH

I was born very weak and small, just five pounds, and spent first two weeks of my life in a Brandish Children's Hospital, correcting a blood disease. I had to have a complete blood transfusion. When my mother brought me home from the hospital she put me in a shoe box because of my size. My grandfather said, "He will never live. He's too small." I proved him wrong. When I was eight months old, mom said I liked to hang like a monkey in my play pen. Mom jokingly told her friends that the blood they transfusion was from a monkey!

My two brothers were much bigger and stronger. To build coordination and muscles, at the age of seven or eight, my mother enrolled me in dance class. In class, we learned basic dance, tumbling, and then tap and soft shoe movements. After a few weeks of practice the teacher thought we should have a recital. I can remember my class;

I was the only boy amongst six girls with me in the middle, putting on this dance recital dressed in tap shoes, a black top hat with a silver ribbon, and a silvery and black costume, with a cane. We danced a routine to the song, Alley Cat. I still remember the steps, believe it or not. Mom was right. I got a little stronger both in muscles and stage performance.

I eventually grew up as a tall, lanky boy with blond hair and very little body hair at that. I was always small built. When I turned 21 years old, I weighed just 121 pounds! I'm 69 years old now, still slim built, five feet, 10 inches tall and 142 pounds.

MY LIFE AS A KID IN THE 50S AND 60S

If you remember me telling you, I would take change from Mom's pocket book. Most of the time I would venture into the pantry when I first got home from school to get loose change to go to the corner store for a treat. Every two or three blocks in my neighborhood there was a small corner store. At the end of my street was Saint Martin's' Store. Two blocks north was Chicago Beef and Produce Store where they sold meats and veggies, and one block south was Patty's Store. I usually went to Bakon's, but each store had its specialties. Sometimes my mother or father would send me to Bakon's to buy cigarettes, bread or milk. Most of these items were 20 to 25 cent each in those days. I guess you're thinking about a kid seven or eight years old buying cigarettes but it was different back then. Everyone knew everybody by their first name and especially, who your parents were which eliminated any problem. Once in a while there would be a spare nickel to spend on candy or an ice cream. They had real one cent candy like Bazooka, Tootsie Rolls, squirrel nut or root beer barrels and other candies that aren't politically correct today. For three cents, you could get a box of Necco Wafers, life savers or hot balls, candy lips, or two Mary Jane's.

For five cents you could get a Charleston Chew candy bar, a box of Good and Plenty, Nestlé's chocolate bar or a Sky Bar, which was my favorite. It didn't take much change to get a treat. The stores had all kinds of gum like: Juicy Fruit, Teaberry, Clove gum and Wrigley's Spearmint, just to name few. My brother and I would get a small brown paper bag of candy and start eating it as soon as we left the store. By the time we got home, five or six houses away, all our candy would be gone. David and I became addicted to sweets at an early age. As we got older, I look back at this habit and realize that it ruined our young teeth and we paid dearly for our love for sweets.

The man, who ran Bakon's Store, collected coins and dollar bills which were displayed all around the store, attached to the top shelf's valance. Sometimes we would find a different coin around our house and he would make us a special deal to secure this coins. Little did I know that they were Buffalo nickels, Indian head and wheat pennies, Standing Liberty quarters, German coins my father brought back from the war, and Mercury dimes which were all collected in those days by coin collectors. Sadly, I can't get them back now for my collections.

We were lucky to have our grammar school just across the street from Bakon's store. We walked to school; crossed the street with a crossing guard and had a playground where we could hang out and play games. Most neighborhoods had their own schools and over the big hill was High School. We had sidewalks on every street to walk to school and crosswalks. I lived in town so I never took a bus to any school all the way through into high school. Just three blocks towards downtown was the town common where in the winter time, we could slide down its hill on our sleds. We were lucky to be able to walk to everything. We only had one car in those days and my mother didn't work or drive and stayed home with us kids.

When I was about nine, and my brother Aiden was 16 years old, he had a clunker of a car that he was always playing with. He would take me to Sam's Junk Yard and we'd walked around looking for parts that he needed to fix his car. He always sent me off on a quest alone or with a friend to find a car like his, while he also searched and had fun with his friends. I got to explore and learned about cars, their year, make and models, along with their differences. In those days every car was unique. You could not only tell a Chevy from a Ford, or a Dodge from a Hudson, but, you would also know what year it was! All cars were not painted silver or white like cars of today. They were, blue, red, white, green, black and yellow.

One time at the junk yard, I heard my brother off in the distance calling out for me, Sandy, Sandy, where are you?!! But he couldn't find me. I had fallen asleep in the front seat of an old Ford coupe, and thought it was a dream. Those days, they let you roam around by yourself and take your own parts out. Sam the owner knew my father and always treated us fairly, sometime no charge. Times do change. Nowadays, when you go to a salvage place it is like a supermarket. You go in, give them the info of the type of vehicle and part and they look it up on a computer and then if they have it, it comes out in 5 minutes ready to go! You have the part, but the fun of the hunt has disappeared.

My mother decided that if her oldest son got his driver's license when he was 16, than she should get her driver's license too, just in case she needed to drive. She was 36 years old.

Rambling around junk yards prompted my interest in cars and mechanical and electrical things at an early age. Our local dump was about a mile away and we would take a ride with my mother to empty the trash there. We'd roam around for a few minutes and find treasures to take home to play with, or as I had mentioned before, Mom would drive us to the town dump, leave us off for an hour or so, and pick us up after her errand. My treasures were always machinery or electrical. I would bring them home, take them apart, put them back together and see how they worked and sometimes fix them. We lived in the days when parents didn't have to worry about their children being taken by a stranger. We never worried about getting hurt or being abducted in those days. Our neighborhoods were close knit; everyone knew you, where you lived, and who your parents were.

My father was always trying to fix our black and white television set so I would collect an assortment of vacuum tubes from old discarded TV's and have them tested at our local TV and radio store, Grozny's. With him and my tubes I learned how to fix televisions and radios at an early age. Grozny always gave me hints. Eventually, our cellar was full of items and we had to bring a few back, but many we kept for years as trophies. This is where I honed my ability to fix things and not be shy when taking something apart; these adventures shaped my mechanical aptitude and my future occupational careers in electronics.

I grew up in an Italian neighborhood with a lot of boys. We road bikes, took hikes, made club houses, played with bugs and reptiles and plagued the few of the girls around. One time we read a flyer from a super-market five miles away that had lemon, banana, chocolate, or coconut pies for sale for 25 cents each. This was enough for all of us to take a hike to the store via backyards and railroad tracks to get our pies. We picked one of each pie flavor, and went out doors to eat our treats. None of us boys had ever shopped at a supermarket by ourselves and didn't realize that the pies were frozen. We ate and shared them anyway! Another time, a McDonald's restaurant had just opened in a town about 15 miles away. They had hamburgers for 15 cents and cheeseburgers for 19 cents. That's all we had to know and took off on our bikes. We ate and rested and decided that we didn't want to bike home, so I called my father from a 10 cent pay phone and he reluctantly came after us boys. Other times, we boys would hike three or four streets away, through the woods and peoples' yards to find our favorite swamp, 'Duckies'. We would collect frogs and turtles, play hide-in-seek, get all muddy and wet and have our packed lunch in the woods like explorers. I still remember our adventures and our wet clothes and shoes when we walked back. Our feet and sock would be black with mud!

The 1960's came along with all kinds of new devices and toys. By the late 60's, color TVs were in most houses along with dishwashers, fluorescent lamps, and of course, the famous trip to the moon which I proudly took a black and white photo of the landing off the television with my Polaroid instant camera to mark this historic event. Turning a teenager was a special event in the 60's. The transistor was invented at Bell Labs and became the new future in electronics. Radios could be smaller and reasonable priced for everyone. I remember my first three transistors, AM radio which could receive two local channels in the daytime and a Boston radio station in the evening. It was amazing! We also had earphones that could be packed in your knapsack for the beach or a hike. Who would think? Of course, I had to take the radio apart to see what made it work. It was 'space-aged' man, compared to vacuum tubes!

I was hooked. I saw an advertisement in the back of 'Boy's Life Magazine' for making your own portable walkie-talkies called 'Space Phones'. You could talk up to a ¼ of a mile away and listen further with its sensitive, super-regenerative receiver. I took my time, read the direction, assembled the parts on a crude circuit board, soldered them together and, "They Worked!" the first time I tried them! I was amazed! Sort of like Dick Tracy. One time, I hiked up to Mount Washington's summit with my brother Aiden and our scout troop and took my Space Phone with me; we were able to talk to a man 25 miles away in Maine. These event and others landed me in college studying electronics in the late '60's and '70's.

Early in my teens, I liked girls but was shy. My mom sent me to Dorothy Helderkins' dance class to learn ballroom dancing. It was great to dance with a different girl during the classes. After dance class, some of us guys would go to the local soda shop which had those stools that spun around. They sold Coke-a-Cola, which could be made with any flavored syrup you wanted like: strawberry, vanilla or cherry, and mixed with soda water. So you could have a cherry or vanilla coke or any combination of flavors. Drinks were 25 cent and French fries were 75 cents and big enough to share with your friends. We had two soda shops like that in town.

I took to dancing and my teacher asked me to come back the next year to help her teach dance. I'm not sure if she needed more boys or I was a good dancer. Well, that year, I met my first 'girlfriend', Michelle. She lived in a town about 18 miles away. So yep, I pedaled my bike to her town to find her house but I could not find it. I guessed she had moved or I had spelled her last name incorrectly. Again, I road my bike back home 18 miles. These classes gave me confidence that I could dance, and dance well. I still teach dance today and in the past, I have run a dance camp for about eight years. Not ballroom dancing but, folk dancing.

Our town had teenage dances at the local park until 10 p.m. on summer, weekend nights. It was fun and gave me more confidence. I went to all the dances at our high school and would always ask a girl to dance even if I didn't know her. Sometimes, I think I was showing off or got a rush from this experience. Whatever it was, it was great.

One night, with three of my friends and my brother Aiden, we decided to go to a dance in another town, Clintons, Massachusetts. We got together and thought we would all dress alike. We decided to wear white fishnet sweaters; maybe we were trying to mimic a popular singing group. I didn't have one, but my friend had an extra, so I wore his. None of us had ever been to this town.

We found the dance at the high school next to an old fire station. We went in and the girls were on one side and the boys were on their side. We tried to mingle and talk until the music started. Then to our surprise, no one got up to danced. So we went over and each of us asked a girl to dance, and we broke the ice. During a break, the boys started talking loudly and warned us to stay away from their girls. We didn't know what to do. One of the girls came up to us and said that we should leave if we knew what was best for us. We took her advice and started to leave, but to our surprise, all the guys followed behind us outside. We walked faster and they did too. Once outdoors we came into a common area. They started pushing us around and threatening us, "Stay away from our girls if you know what's good for ya!" Then they started to get excited and pushing us boys around. I guess they were testing our response to their threats! Then, me and one my friends got pushed to the ground and beat up! They began kicking and punching us all over. One of our guys ran to the fire station and got an elderly fireman who was on call to come out and he tried to break up the fight.

One of our 'other' friends pretended that he was one of the guys from Clinton and stood around watching us get beat up. I remember hearing him yell during all the commotions, "Get those guys, they're trying to take our girls!" What a rat! By the time it ended, three of us were covered with blood all over our white sweaters and received stern advice from the fireman, "Get the hell out of town NOW!" We ran back; I mean ran, to our car in disbelief. We started the car, rolled the windows up, locked the doors and got the hell out of Clinton. To this day, if I have to travel through Clinton, I still keep my windows up. We made it back to Marlboro and the only place open at that time of night was, Dunkin' Donuts. We went straight into the bathroom, compared our injuries and cleaned up as best we could so we could sneak into our homes. I got home, and tried to quietly go upstairs to my bedroom. Mom noticed that something was different and whispered, "Are you OK?" I said, "Yah..." Well the rest is history.

So these years shaped my life forever. A career in electronics; able to fix most anything, dance all night and every dance and the ability to reflect on all these adventures I had and still have!

REMEMBERING CHRISTMAS

Looking back to the years before I turned ten, my brother David, who was three years younger, shared the same bedroom. It was a boy's room with Lone Ranger wallpaper with 'Hi Oh Silver, Away' and two single beds. My bed was next to the window and David's was by the wall. I especially remember Christmas time on the night before Christmas. My brother David and I sat on my bed with our feet on the baseboard heat gazing out the window as to catch a glimpse of Santa Clause. The windows faced north so it was the ideal vantage point for looking towards the North Pole. We would look for what seemed hours and either fall asleep in the same bed or get frustrated by not seeing Santa. We would look for the North Star, UFO's, fireworks or whatever fired our young imaginations at the time. I'm sure our parents came in and checked on us and finding us both asleep in the same bed, moved us to our separate beds. We did this for years and this picture is still clear in my mind.

We would hang our stockings on a string with clothes pins in front of an old built-in hutch in the dining room. We didn't have a fireplace, so we improvised. This hutch held all of our boyhood treasures like rocks, coins, stamps, experiments and baseball cards and at the time seemed like the most treasured spot in the house and the one that Santa was sure to go to. Looking back, I wish I had kept all those baseball cards from the 50's and 60's instead of putting them on our bikes to make a loud noise; they would probably be valuable today. We were allowed to get up in the morning and open our stockings but nothing under the tree until our parents got up and had their coffee.

We always received the typical things like candy, small toys, Silly

Putty, and some fruit in out stockings. We couldn't wait to open our presents and share our joys with each other. We peeked at the names on the presents under the tree but never dared to open any of them. Occasionally, we would give them a gentle shaking to see if we could figure out what was in the package. One year, I got a Mr. Robot who strolled along the floor, made a noise and blinking lights. It was just what I wanted. Another year, I received a make-your-own radio station. You had to build it. I built it and my neighbor and I got it to transmit all the way down our street on our 3 transistor portable AM radio. I had my own radio station! I put antennas all over the yard to see if I could get more coverage. The next year I received a build-your-own 'Spacephone' walkie-talkie kit. These were the ones I told you about previously. These presents brought me hours of joy.

Our Christmases weren't without mishaps. One year the dog pulled the tree over and broke all of our special antique ornaments. They had been in the family for 60 years. My mother just reminded me of this and added that, "Your father put the tree in a play pen and tied it up with string to prevent that from happening again." Then, she also told this story.

"One year, the dog took from under the Christmas tree, a half-gallon glass bottle of gin, the type with the handle on its side and proceeded to carry it from the living room, into the kitchen. Well, she dropped it on the floor and broke it. The dog ended up cutting her foot and we had to bring her to the vet to have her foot repaired." I wonder now if the dog was trying to tell our parents something.

Another time, the day after Christmas, while building a snow fort, I accidentally hit my dog's head with the shovel. This made me and Aiden very sad because she looked at me with those hurt eyes as if to say, "Why did you hit me?" That bothered me for a long time. I didn't mean to hurt her, but how could I tell her that? Maybe she understood by the tone of my voice.

We would go to Grandma's house for dinner or they would come to our house. My grandmother would always make ambrosia with: pineapple, miniature marshmallows, coconut and cherries. My aunt would always give her nephews a brand new, crisp one dollar bill in one of those envelopes that you'd opened and could see Washington's face. When I turned 13, she gave me a crisp new five dollar note!

After dinner we would fight for one of the two couches and watch a football game, movie or a parade. I would fall asleep every time after eating so much turkey. Turkey does that to me especially if you were known to have hollow legs. I would have to sample all the deserts you know. Now that I have children and they have children, these traditions have been passed on, creating memories that they will look back on as I am doing now.

GIRLS AND SEX

My father always had a part-time job as a janitor at our neighborhood Congregational neighborhood church. Naturally, we became members of the church and attended Sunday school and summer church camp. One year, David and I went to summer day camp, he was around nine and I was 11-12. There was a boy's tent and a girls' tent, and we took our lunches and rode a bus back and forth. The camp was situated on Fort Meadow Lake in Marlboro, Massachusetts. Being young and curious boys, we were also enchanted by being away from home and spending time with the girls. We had no sisters so it was an oddity and a treat for us. We learned how to swim, play horseshoes, sit around a campfire to roast marshmallows and paddle a canoe.

One day, right after swimming classes, a few of us boys quietly snuck over to the side of girl's tent. We slowly and quietly knelt down €©¹on the ground and lifted a corner of the tent so we could watch the girls change out of or into their bathing suit. I can't remember if we ever saw anything, but I do remember we got caught! They said it was Sandy's idea! Girls were new to us; they were different than boys and teased us by having secrets and trying to kiss us.

Every summer our family would go to my grandfather's cottage in Maine, but sometimes we would stay in town at their big old house and sleep together upstairs. There was an old attic off our room and David and I would tip-toe in it and look at all the treasures. Once we found some National Geographic magazines from the 1940's. We would sneak them into our room and look at the naked native people. We never knew there were such magazines to be had, but finally, we got to see our first naked women. From that point on, we looked at girls differently.

Our neighbors had a garage and we would hang out there and play hide-n-seek, Cowboy and Indians and spin-the-bottle, but we also wanted our own place to hang out. Dad was a painter in those days and managed to salvage some old wood from a job, and window shutters with cutout shapes of pine trees on their top section. Using these shutters, he helped us make our very own 'club house' under one of our big pine trees. It was neat. Mom would make us a lunch and we would lie on the ground and eat pretending that we were on a desert island or cowboys in a hideout. Now we had our own spin-the-bottle place, too! Coming of age for me was sort of a mystery. My mom gave each of her sons the same book at different stages in our lives. It was called, *All You Wanted to Know About Sex, but Didn't Want to Ask*. She kept it in our attic on a shelf off of our bedroom and told us we should all read it. And we did! We would take it to the club house and read and look at the pictures.

Once one of the neighborhood boys took a girly magazine from his uncle and snuck it into our fort so we could all look at it. It was amazing and answered some of those unasked questions. Now, I probably shouldn't tell you this story, but, it is a part of our growing up. Before we went into puberty we boys would take hikes into the woods and take our clothes off and run around the woods and jump and climb trees like early cave men did. We never did anything weird but were curious and exchanged stories. Sure, we kissed girls once in a while and kind of hugged them from the side, but that was it at least for me.

Most of the time, dancing with a girl was as close as we got. I can still remember the awkwardness, sweaty hands and the slight smell of a girl's clothes and body. It was alluring and release chemicals in my body and imprinted images in my mind's eye. I was starting to grow some light blond hair on my boyish body in places where it never grew before.

On one summer morning, while sleeping on my stomach, I had a vivid dream about a girl who had kissed me at camp that week. I had strange unconscious energy explosions in my dream which half woke me up, but I laid there and tried to go back to sleep to see if this feeling would return. It did come back once more, but this time, I woke up with the front of my pajamas all wet. What was going on? Well of course I know now. That was my first wet dream! For that whole week I tried to recreate these magical feelings and it happened two more times. I was entering adolescence!

BOYS WILL BE BOYS

We had a lot of girlfriends in our neighborhood. Most of the time we plagued the girls and tried to gross them out. One time we caught a snake and decided that I should ride my bike up the road and when I passed the other boys, yes, in front of the girls, they would throw the snake into the spokes of my bicycle to cut up the snake. "I'm sorry Mister Snake, forgive me!"

Another time we were catching grasshoppers and the girls dared us to eat one. I guess I was kind of like Mikey, in those TV commercials, the boy who would do anything. I took their dare, and ate the grasshopper by first taking its wings off and squeezing the back half behind the head and chewing this half right in front of everyone. The girls couldn't believe it.

About a mile from our house was a dairy farm we would cut through on our way to the town dump. We would cut through the fields because it was shorter, and gave us more time to play MOOing with the cows. In our group there was one boy who was the oldest, only by two weeks of me. He always bullied us into things that we would not have done if we were by ourselves. There was an electric fence around the cows to keep them in and he dared me to pee on the fence. Well, I had never seen an electric fence or knew of its potential. I should have studied electricity in school more seriously. I pulled it out and started to pee on the fence. With the first shot I missed. He said, "Get closer, it won't hurt you." I could see no harm, and got closer. On my second try, I hit the edge of the wire with my stream. You all know what happened! That electricity came right up my liquid stream and into my penis shocking the shit out of me. From that point on, I learned to respect electricity and not to pee on electric fences.

As a very young boy I had a peeing problem. I would stand in front of the toilet for a while to pee. My mother tricked me into a way of speeding up the process. She would run the water in the bathroom sink until it made a whistling sound. It worked like a charm. I trained myself to run the water myself in order to pee. Well, it worked then, but now, I have the curse. To this day, whenever I run water or even pump gas, I have the uncontrollable urge to pee. I just found out a while ago that my 92 year-old mothers had the same urge when she ran water. Her parents must have taught her this trick.

There was an old shoe factory right behind our house on a small dead end road. We always cut through the alleys to go over there to look for treasures. On the back side of the factory was a loading dock and across the dirt road there was a small wooded area and a junkyard with all kinds of metal objects. It was a great place to play when the factory was deserted.

One day when I was 11, we boys were exploring on the loading dock, and we found an empty square five gallon metal container with the cap on. I shook it and to my surprise, something jiggled inside like a coin or something similar. All us boys were curious and stood around as I took the cap off. Looking down the hole, I could see it was metal and about the size of a silver half-dollar. I couldn't see exactly what was inside because the light wasn't right. Someone suggested that I could use a match to see what was inside. One of us young boys would always have a match in our pocket. I lit the match, looked into the hole and dropped the match inside. "Puff!" it exploded and burned all the hair on my head and my eyebrows also! I'll never forget the smell of burning hair and the rawness of my skin from the explosion. I was scared! The other kids ran off and I ran home alone terrified of the event and what was to come when I got there. My mother was shocked and called my dad at work so he could come home and take us to our doctor. The doc said that there was no permanent damage and he gave us some salve to apply and said to keep it covered and clean. I was embarrassed to go to school that Monday with a bandage and a hat on. Aiden told all his friends and they called me 'Come-head"! I had to keep it on all week until hair finally began to slowly grow back. "Accidents" do happen, but I can remember I faked an event because I was too embarrassed to face what I had done. I was 13 years old and going off to my first teenage school dance, I was getting all clean and spruced up for my first teenage dance. I took a shower and washed my neck, ears and face, along with shampooing my hair. Before I put my jacket on, I spent a few minutes in front of my fathers' shaving mirror making faces and trying to comb my hair so it didn't stick up in the back. Mom told me that it stuck up because I had two crowns on my head; that meant that I could part my hair on either side of my head, big deal; but it always stuck up in the back. These were the times I felt like Alfalfa from the Little Rascals, and I surely didn't need another nickname.

My father's shaving mirror was so high of the ground that all I could see was my hair sticking up when both my feet were on the ground. I devised a way to see in the mirror by placing one foot on the side of the bathtub and one knee on the sink, but I still had to hold on with one hand to balance myself. I finally realized that to rectify my problematic hair, I had to trim it, but, I was trying to cut my hair with the wrong hand, and that didn't work. To fix this problem, I stood on my tip-toes, looked in the mirror, where I could only view the top inch of my hair on my head, and cut a little off and it worked. The next week I went out again to a dance, so I cut a little more off to even it out. Eventually, it was perfect.

One day my mother asked me, "What is happening to your hair?" "It looks like a crew cut!" I told her "I don't know what had happened, Mom, really!" "Maybe I have a hair disease or something!" Once again, I went to the doctor, this time for a lotion to make my hair grow. Of course I knew what had happened, but I was too ashamed to tell anyone in fear of getting punished with another whipping. Well, I kept this secret for 22 years, and the day my father died, I told my mother the truth. I still feel guilty that they had to pay for another doctor's visit and also that I had lied to my mother. All these events helped to shaped me into being a 'Renaissance Man', but I guess probably I could have done it an easier and less harmful way.

As a young boy, I liked to go fishing with my grandfather. I remember getting up early and traveling to a pond where my grandfather had his rowboat stored. We'd fish for a while and we'd get hungry. My grandmother, who was a great baker, would pack homemade biscuit or donuts for our snacks. Grandpa would always have a thermos of hot instant coffee with some PM (Perfect Moment) Whiskey added to take the chill off. I can remember tasting this concoction and it was great!

As the morning progressed, we'd nibble the food and drink some coffee while fishing. I wondered to myself, where can I go pee. I held it as long as I could because I didn't want Grandpa to row back to shore. I finally got up the courage to ask him what I should do. He said to me, "Stand up in the boat and pee off the side!" I was shy but he assured me it would be ok. To make me feel better he said, "It will attract the fish!"

My brother and I would go on daily adventures while vacationing in Maine. One day, we decided to take a walk to the candy store by cutting though nearby yards. We came upon an ornate brick outdoor barbeque with a four-foot chimney. I had the bright idea to test out the theory that Santa Clause could fit down the chimney to deliver our presents. I climbed up on top; put both legs in and slid to the bottom. I made it to the fire chamber and decided it was possible. When, I tried to get out ...yep, I was stuck! My brother tried to get me out but I was definitely STUCK. We decided that he should go back to my grandfather's house to get help. My father and uncle came to the rescue. After a few words were exchanged they got me out of the chimney. I could see a little laughter on their faces as they shook their heads.

A not so funny thing happened to me when I was eight years old. My 5 year old brother Aiden was a little husky when he was younger and enjoyed eating. One day, my mother went to the corner store for groceries and left the two of us alone in the house with me in charge. My brother decided that he wanted to open a new box of cereal instead of eating the box that was opened. As the person in charge, I insisted that he stop and eat the cereal that was already opened. He got mad at me and started to open the new box anyway with a pair of scissors that was on the counter. I told him to stop and began taking the box away from him. Enraged, He picked up the scissors he had used to open the new box, and stabbed me in the back. The blood came gushing out and we panicked. I took off my belt and put it around the wound with a towel against the opening. He knew he was in big trouble. We both looked out the window to see if my mother was walking back from the store. After awhile, she started back. She came in and saw my state and Doug was hiding in the corner with a bright red face and shaking his head saying, "It was an accident, I didn't mean to do it!" Mom called my father again and he came home from work and took me to the doctors. He cleaned it, took x-rays, and gave me a shot. The scissors had punctured my lung but not too far in. Well my brother got his punishment and to this day I can still feel the place where the scissors entered my back. I forgive my brother!

FIRST 'DAYS' OF SCHOOL

I want to warn you ahead of time before you read this section that these following events are true and were very traumatic to me as well as embarrassing. School was always stressful for me, especially, 'first days' of school each year with a new teacher, subjects, kids and environment. I say "Days" because it happened many 'first days' to me. I usually choose a seat in the middle of the others but a lot of time I didn't have a choice and was stuck in the front or the very back of the classroom. I was a small, frail kid, with light blond hair and complexion, and most of my classmates were Italian or Greek. I had to feel out the situations with our new teacher and our subjects. All teachers were not the same and different rules did apply. It always made me nervous.

In second grade I was only six years old, and my mother felt that I was too young to advance because of my reading skills. So she convinced the school that I should stay back and repeat second grade to improve my reading skills. It did help but, I had to get used to a new set of classmates that I didn't know! This made me more nervous even though, I had the same teacher, but I got through the year without too much trauma.

Our new third year teacher was very strict and you could tell that she had no children by the way she treated us students; not as individuals, but a person to keep inline. With all my nervous conditions at the beginning of school, I asked permission from this teacher a lot to go to the bathroom but, many times she would deny me my request. I never took advantage of this privilege but she treated us all the same. Now I've never told anyone this story but it is true. After so many times of being denied to go to the bathroom, I developed a way of coping with my situation. Likely my seat was in the center of the class toward the back and people paid less attention to me. This was in the early 1950's and we had those wooden desks with the ink well on the top right corner and instead of a top that opened up, we had an opening the length of the front facing me. Inside my desk I had books, papers, writing materials and a small 6x8 inch cardboard box with a lift off cover that contained our letters to make words on our desk. Being desperate at times, I found that instead of asking to go the bathroom I would edge this box of letters toward the opening of my desk and prop up the top slightly. Then, looking all over the room and waiting for the perfect moment, I would secretly unzipped my pants and sneak my penis into this opening just slightly. Then I'd look all around or wait for another focal point and release the aching pressure just slightly enough to get me through to the end of class when I could finish this deed. Well, needless to say, by the end of the year, my letter box was terrible smelling and falling apart from the consistent moister. Being totally consumed with embarrassment, I just left it in the desk when I moved onto the next grade. What else could I do?

I recall another story similar to the one above. We lived in an old house which only had one bathroom downstairs. My mom grew up in the 20s and they had the same bathroom configuration. In her house they took a chamber pot to bed which came in quite handy on those cold winter nights. Well, in our house we called them 'pee cans', everyone had one next to their bed. Well, they would get used and would end up every day with pee in them. Pretty normal I guess. Our third grade teacher asked us students what responsibilities we performed at home. When it got to be my turn, I innocently told the teacher that, "It was my turn to empty the 'pee cans' and wash them out." Well that afternoon my teacher called my mother at home and asked her what this was all about and she told her the story! I never heard any more about this story.

As I think back, I always had a peeing problem. When the school day ended, we were all ushered out in a line and sent home which didn't give me time to relieve myself. I would rush home as fast as I could and run around our house to the back and under the clothes line, up against the house, I would go the bathroom. I knew I couldn't hold it any longer; sometimes it was really bad because I would prolong my misery by stopping at the candy store on the way home. As I got older, my mother said that she always would know when I was home from school because she would see me run past the kitchen window on my way out back to pee!

Don't get grossed out but this did happen to me. You have to do what you have to do if you can't control it! Well, another incident happened the first day of 7th grade, junior high. It was a new building to me, and for the first time we had to move from class to class and again, my system was nervous. I guess I didn't have time to go poop that morning properly and with all the daily movements of classes it aggravated my condition. On the first day of school we were bombarded by all that information and rules and no teacher would ever think of letting you leave class to go the bathroom on the first day. Well, I starting having pains in my belly and I knew that I had to poop. Suddenly, I couldn't hold it any longer and I went a little in my pants to relieve the pressure. I sat all through class with this small load in my pants unable to concentrate on class matters. As soon as the bell rang, I started off to my next class area. I had to go up two flights of stairs winding around the corners, to the next landings with people all around me doing the same thing; some going up, some going down. Suddenly, to my surprise while going from a landing to the next set of stairs, a small perfectly round piece of poop worked its way down my pant leg and fell out onto the landing. Other kids saw it and I turned back and exclaimed, "Oh, I must have a hole in my pocket, there goes one of my 'malted milk balls' again!" I got away with it but before my next class, in the bathroom I took time to clean up myself and threw out my underwear and also went back to clean up the 'malted' milk ball! Gross, but I had no choice. There were other times but these stories were the most notable!

When I went to high school things changed and got much better. No more 'First days' to curse me. I was very technical inclined and joined the audio/visual club. This let me out of my classes anytime I wanted too to run movies and audio equipment. What a relief!! I could use the bathrooms without being denied.

School wasn't so bad after all. I joined the band and played trumpet. I wasn't the best but musician but I tried. I can remember our band leader saying, "Did you practice Mr. Willett"? (He caught me!) There were benefits to being in the band. You got to go to all the football games and march from the field to the Main Street when we won. I vividly remember my freshman year because we did some exciting things. One thing we did was have a guest celebrity come to the school, Myron Florin, who played the accordion with Lawrence Whelk and together, we put on a show for the town. Another time we traveled to New York City in 1964 and played at the World's Fair. That was a ball; we had a hotel room like on the 8th floor and would open the window and act up. 1964 was a big year for building infrastructure in Marlboro and they had just completed the final section of road for our new interstate highway, Route 495 and the governor flew in on a helicopter and we played a couple of song at the dedication. These are things you tell your kids when you go by these places I guess. I was also in the school chorus and did shows during holidays. We had a great time and built lasting friendships.

So, I guess, if I were to sum up all these instances and evaluate them, I should have done it differently. From the beginning, when being too shy to ask to go the bathroom, I should have let my parents know what was happening so they could support me with my problems by calling the school. Remember the parents pay the teachers.

SHH! MASTURBATION

Summer was coming, and I decided to go away for my first week-long, overnight church camp with members of my youth group. This would be the first overnight camp with boys and girls together; before this I went to Boy Scout camp for a few years. The boys were housed in three, big, old, army surplus canvas tents that were very hot during the summer days, and cold in the evenings. I believe the girls were in a dormitory. Our days were chockfull of activities as well as chores. We had chores to facilitate cooking, cleaning and religious presentations which we all had to take part in. We swam, rowed boats, paddled canoes and had campfires with stories and skits.

There was not a lot of down time except in the afternoons when we had free swimming activities. One day, while walking to my tent with a friend, who was slightly older, he told me to remind him that he had something to show me this week; a secret! "Ok," I said, and we went back to our tent. I believed he was working on a plan to make time when we could be alone so he could tell me his secret. He decided that we both should skip free swimming class the next day, "OK." I said.

It was wicked hot, and we were sweating because we hadn't gone for a cool swim. The tent slept 10-12 kids on old folding army cots arranged along the outside of the tent wall with a small clear area in the center for pow-wows. We both sat on his cot in our bathing suits, and he said he wanted to show me what he had learned from one of his friends back home. Before he showed me, he took one last look out the canvas door to see if the coast was clear. It was!

While keeping a low profile on his cot, he wiggled out of his bathing suit and told me to do the same. We sat there on his army cot naked, all alone in that big tent. I reached for my towel on my cot and covered myself because I was shy and didn't know what was going to happen next. Maybe we were going to play twist-the-towel and run around the tent naked while trying to snap each other's butt with the end of the towel No, I was wrong.

He got quiet, looked around the tent once more while listening to the activities off at the lake, and then, he started to touch his penis and stroke it back and forth. He began to talk about girls at camp describing their features, and told me to do the same as he was and it would help. Help what?

Well, magically his penis got bigger and bigger, and he showed me how to hold my penis and stroke it. Kind of strange, but mine also got bigger too! He kept stroking his penis harder and faster and told me to do the same, and suddenly, all this white, sticky stuff shot out of the end of his penis all over his belly and chest just like a squirt gun! While panting and short of breath, and gasping in ecstasy, he said to me, "Keep doing it faster and move your hand down towards your balls and squeeze the shaft a little while stroking." Then it happened to me! The magical white, milky fluid shot out of the end of my penis and this magical sensation went from my member to my head, down my spine and into my mouth with, "WOW! What was that?" The feeling lasted for a long time.

Now I knew what that magical feeling was I had felt one time while sleeping on my stomach, and waking up all wet. It was the same feeling, but I was awake this time. It was amazing and I never knew this was inside the part of me where I also went peed from! Well, we must have secretly met five times that week so we could practice our new treat. "Wow!" I learned how to masturbate at church camp!

I guess you thought it would end there, but it didn't. When I got home, I could not wait to tell my best friend Mack about camp; I told him I had to show him something secret and I couldn't tell him at his home. So we went over to his grandmother's house which used to be a mini farm in the old days. There was an abandoned chicken coop on the property. We looked around. The coast was clear, and we sat on the floor in a corner so as not to be seen. It was hot in there like my first time in the tent at camp, but it smelled completely different. He had no idea what I was going to tell, him.

I showed him what I learned at summer camp. We sat next to each other and I instructed him to pull down his pants like I did and follow my instructions. He was frightened at first, but after a while, he got the hang of it and he too shot his secret white liquid and experienced that hard-to-describe feeling that runs through your whole body and lasts for a half an hour. Over the week, we tried it a couple times so he could do it on his own. Eventually he showed his cousin, and his cousin showed his neighbor, and so on. Mack asked, "What did we start?"

I wonder how it all happened to you and what your story is. I assume it may not be as colorful as my experience, and probably more private, but maybe it was. **Another fact that I can pass on to you younger guys is, "Don't Worry!" As a kid, you hear, "You are going to go blind or wear 'it' out if you do that too much!" I'm 69 years old now, and it still works just fine and still gives me much**

enjoyment and pleasure. I always believed that it was good for my health and heart, and clears my mind. My pulse is always 60 beats per minute; I have 100% oxygen in my blood, and low blood pressure! What else could you ask for? Then I found out what girls were for...

CIRCUMCISION AND VASECTOMY

As far as I know, in the olden days, all the male relatives on my father's side were not circumcised and maybe on my mother's side as well. In the 1940's and '50's male children were not routinely circumcised. When I was nine years old and in third grade, we had a doctor visit our class and give the girls and boy's physicals (separately of course). The doctor took his temperature readings and blood pressure readings and looked into our mouths and ears. We were in our underwear and for the first time in my life he looked in our pants and told us to turn our heads and cough. He didn't say anything to me other than, "next". A few days later he called all the parents with the results and when he called my mother he told her that I should be circumcised because found it has been found to be more hygienic. I wonder if I was secretly born Turkish where boys were circumcised between the ages of five and puberty. Mom contacted my family doctor and he agreed with the first doctor. I had no idea what was involved or how much pain and suffering it would cause me or its advantages.

My mother scheduled the operation and I went to the hospital. They put me out and performed the task. When I woke up, I was sick to my stomach and throwing up and sore in my crotch. My penis was covered in a two inch thick, round bandage made of cotton and tape with a little hole on the end to pee though.

It was really sore and when I went home, my mom had to change my dressings often. One special moment comes to mind when my mother invited her girlfriend over to witness the changing of the dressings. It was embarrassing even at nine years old. As I grew older my penis grew larger. If you were to look at it now, when I am erect, you would see three long stitches at the end of my penis. The head is skewed to the right so I never pee straight without orientating my body at a 45-degree angle to the side of a toilet. The good thing that came from it was that most women I have had sex with fancied a circumcised man. As far as I know, I'm the only one in my family who was circumcised. When my son was born in 1976, it was common practice for him to be circumcised.

In 1979 I was working for MIT and we had just had the birth of our daughter. We had planned to have a boy and girl and we did. We used the book, 'How to Choose the Sex of Your Baby' and it worked. Our second baby was a girl. The procedure was complicated and calculated to make it all work in our favor. I had to cut out coffee, eat well and time my connection according to my wife's cycle. I was on a business trip out west and my wife called me to announce that I had about 48 hours to time the connection so we would have a girl. It all has to do with the life existence of the X and Y chromosomes or something like that. The rest is history and we ended up with a boy and a girl.

I decided I wanted a vasectomy, so we would have any accidents and my wife wouldn't have to use messy birth control again. Sometime after my daughter's birth, I contacted an urologist doctor at MIT in Cambridge and asked him if he could perform this operation. He said yes, but he had no facilities at his office, he suggested that a dentist friend of his would let him use his office after hours. Yes, I had the operation in a dentist's chair, after hours and for $50. I was required to shave that area down there before the operation. My wife helped me shave the delicate parts I couldn't see! The entire operation took about 45 minutes. He made two small incisions on each side and placed two plastic clamps over the tubes and sewed them. It was sore for two days but it was worth it because we had the family we wanted, that is a son and daughter, and my wife or I didn't have to use any more birth control.

SCOUTING

My father obtained a new part-time janitor job at another church, so, I became Baptist this time. I had to read the entire bible as a requirement in my Sunday school class and also lead a church service as a requirement for my Boy Scouts 'God and Country' award; I also become a deacon of this church. This scouting award took a whole year to obtain. I vividly remember that my picture was in the local newspaper with my parents and the minister because I had a funny smirk on my face and as a teenager that's the last thing you want to see in the paper if you don't look perfect.

In scouting I learned how to build a fire, pack a pack, hike, sleep outdoors, cook without utensils, keep warm camping in February when it's -20 below zero and I excelled in the merit badge program. Most of all, I learned how to Be Prepared. I swam the mile swim twice, camped out on a cliff by myself over-night, made my food from scratch, stopped talking while working for 24 hours, learned how radios worked and learned boating and canoeing, too.

Every summer our troop would go to scout camp for a week at Camp Resolute in Bolton, Massachusetts. We slept in lean-tos with up to four boys in each. Being only 13 years old, I was a little homesick, but my mother cured that by sending me a card or photo with a dollar spending money in it. That was great! I went to the camp for five years and learned how to get along with other boys, how to follow rules, tackle chores, and learn leadership skills. I eventually made 'Star' scout and a member of the 'Order of the Arrow,' and had a good jump on my future careers.

Order of the Arrow initiation was a big deal for me. I was with other 14 and15 year old boys. To prove our stamina and character, we had to go an whole day without talking, be lead out into the woods to cut a fire trail with just a hatchet (my young hands were all bleeding blisters by the end of the day) and then, we were lead out to a cliff on a dark night with just a sleeping bag and told not to move from that spot. This was the first time I had ever slept under the stars and out in the open without a tent. When daylight came I noticed I was about five feet from the edge of a high rock cliff. I'm glad they told us not to move from our spot. We were not permitted to speak until we went to mess hall for breakfast.

After passing all our initiations, we were able to talk and sleep inside the next night. During this evening, we were woken up by the older scouts, who stripped off our pants and sprayed us with shaving cream. Then they took us by our arms and legs and carried us out to the lake and threw us into the water. The rest of the camp was normal.

I had a lot of great adult mentors that showed me many tricks of the trades. If you have a chance to join the Boy Scout, do it. These experiences have stayed with me, have been invaluable, and prepared me for most events in my life. When we go for a hike or on vacation I can always be counted on to be prepared and have all the necessary items for a safe and productive adventure.

MEDIA: TV, RADIO AND NEWSPAPER

Likes any kid in the '50's I liked to watch TV and listen to the radio. Our first TV, black and white, was a square nine inch screen in a cabinet that was three times that size weighed 50 pounds. On the top and bottom of the screen were brackets. These brackets held a 12 by12 by 4-inch thick convex magnifying glass which made the TV screen seem like it was bigger. We had three channels: WBZ from Boston, where we watched 'Boom Town', 'Big Brother' and The Walt

Disney Show (NBC); channel 5, WHDH, Boston where we watched the 'Three Stooges', 'Abbott and Costello', 'Superman' and 'Little Rascals' (CBS) and, channel 7 WNAC, Boston (ABC) where we watched 'Captain Kangaroo' and The Ed Sullivan Show. Eventually we got channel 2, PBS. In those days we had an antenna on top of the TV that looked like 'Rabbit Ears' and one would have to twist them around to get the best reception for each channel. If you didn't get it just right the screen would turn to horizontal lines and roll up and down zigzag. Televisions in those days had controls for vertical and horizontal hold, brightness and contrast. We eventually updated to a larger TV set.

My father always looked at the Sunday paper for TV deals and would drag us all in to look at the new televisions. He was motivated by sales like, Christmas, Washington's Birthday and Labor Day. Sometimes, Dad would see a TV by the side of the road and pick it up, bring it home, and try to fix it by taking the tubes out and testing them. Sometimes it would work and sometimes it went back to the dump. This is how I learned about fixing TVs as a young lad. I remember getting shocked by the high-voltage coil which goes to the picture tube. Not the first time! I always took things apart, sometimes successfully and sometimes not. Next came the fad of TV console units. They housed a TV, AM/FM radio and a record player all in the same unit! I can remember the TV part eventually wore out and Dad took the TV out, bought a portable one, and set it in the existing opening.

In 1969, Dad bought our first color TV. He saw an ad one on sale in Boston, and we all packed into the Chevy and picked it out. We were lucky in 1969 to see on our color TV Neil Armstrong's walk on the moon, even though it was broadcast in black and white. To document this event, I took a black and white photo off the TV with my Polaroid instant camera. I still have the print!

I had two favorite shows, and as a young kid timed my day around them. Every Sunday night we would take our bath for school the next day, and watch the Walt Disney Show from 8-9 p.m. and the Superman show aired Monday through Friday at five p.m. I always asked to sit in front of the TV to eat my supper but it was not always granted. To this day, I must admit, that I was temporarily in shock when Walt Disney died and Superman killed himself. How could this happen?

Eventually, remote control TVs came out. At first, they were controlled by a button you pushed, and it would emit an auditable chime noise to activate the on and off and channel functions. Before this, hold on to your seats folks, *we had to get off the couch and walk up to the TV to change the channel or adjust the other functions.* Today, everything is controlled remotely, wirelessly, and without any physical activity besides moving a finger, or every one sits on the same couch and watches something different on their hand-held computer. I do like remote controls but I have not yet graduated into the Wi-Fi, I-Pod age.

Radio hasn't changed a much over the years. In the old days, TVs and radios were huge and heavy. They hummed when you turned them on until they warmed up and everything was AM, no stereo or FM. With AM radio, local radio stations would operate from sunrise to sunset and play the National Anthem at both ends of their service day. In the evening, since the local stronger stations were off the air, you could hear stations hundreds of miles away and sometimes as far off as Canada or Mexico. This was exciting and made the earth seem a little smaller and closer.

I was interested in radio as a young kid and went to our local 'AM' radio station, WSRO, and got a tour to see their studio and transmitters. That was super! In 1959, the first portable, three transistor radio came out on the market. I received one for Christmas. It was large, had an antenna that you pulled out, ran on batteries and only had AM reception. You could only get the local channel during the daytime but after sunset, you could get WBZ radio in Boston. Eventually, six transistor units were introduced; and they were more sensitive and louder. In a few more years, FM transmission was invented and music could be transmitted in stereo because of the extended bandwidth.

With recorded music, there were only three choices: the antique 78's which were heavy and thick and only had one song per side; small 45 rpm records, and large, 33 and1/3 rpm long playing records. Eventually, music was recorded on 8-track stereo tapes. I know because we had them in our cars. Next, came cassette tapes with two sides of music to listen to and now, we have CDs, digital keys, and I-Tunes, clouds, etc.

Newspapers always fascinated me. The paper would be delivered to your house, contain news, photos and ads, and people would pay for them. As a child entrepreneur I had the great idea to start my own newspaper. I and two other neighborhood kids joined me in my publishing career. We went down to the local newspaper, the Marlboro Enterprise, for a tour to see how everything went together. They had a reporting office, teletype machines to receive news from faraway places, and typesetting machines where they lined up letters and words embossed on reversible lead blanks to form sentences and articles. It was all amazing. The newspaper was so enthusiastic about our interest, that they took our photos and interviewed us for an article in their newspaper.

Our neighborhood newspaper was named, 'The Local Journal'. We went around on our street and asked people if they had any news for us, like: "Tom Dogan got up too soon and hit his head on a door and had to get a stitch in his head'. We had ads like: Buy Savings Bonds, turn your clocks ahead, Tommy C lost his cat but found him two days later… What we did was take three pieces of paper, with carbon paper between the sheets to make two copies. Then we would repeat the process for the next 10 copies. We sold them to the neighborhood for three cents each and sold out the first week. We did this for two more weeks but then; we lost interest because of the manual efforts involved, but we did it, and experienced the process. I eventually went into delivering newspapers for two seasons and I liked that because at 14 years old, I earned money and got to meet my neighbors.

It was great to have childhood idols and a variety of interests to stimulate our young brains and actions. There was always something to look forward to each week. My advice, try something new for a change...You may like it!

HAM RADIO, ALSO KNOWN AS AMATEUR RADIO

Everyday while walking to school, I passed by a giant 100 foot radio tower that was attached to the side of a house. One day, I met up with the girl who lived there and asked her what the tower was all about. She told me that her father was a radio amateur, a 'Ham,' and she had mentioned that she had a younger brother who was just learning the trade.

I became best friends with her brother, Mitch and we learned how to build radios and repair them from his father. I decided to learn the proper technical side of radio and at 11 years old, I studied radio fundamentals and Morse code to obtain my "Novice" class radio operators license. We began by using his father's equipment to send messages to other ham radio operators all around the world. Eventually, I learned how to read schematics and operate a soldering iron to build radios using discreet components, i.e. resisters, diodes, capacitors, fixed and variable, tubes and transistors. We were limited by the modes and frequencies of our novice class license, so I decided to study for the next licenses class, "Technician". This gave us more latitude and also we could talk using voice instead of using Morse code all the time.

For Christmas one year, I received my first store bought transceiver from Lafayette Radio store, a model HE-45. I talked my father into climbing up on the roof and installing a three element antenna and rotor for the six meter band. I joined the ARRL, 'American Radio Relay League,' like every other ham operator and spent many hours talking or try to reach ham radio operators all over the world. We would exchange 'QSL' cards, which stated your contacts, what kind of equipment you had and where you lived.

My first call was 'KN1ZCU' and when I received my technician class, I was 'K1ZCU'; they dropped the 'N' out of the call to signify I had a higher class of license than the Novice class. I joined the Air Force MARS (Military Affiliated Radio Systems) program which taught me how to pass messages for service men and emergency notifications via radio. This opened up all kinds of free army surplus radio equipment to tinker with. I had a big six foot equipment rack in my bedroom and my mother was afraid to come into my room fearing the wires and electricity. Eventually, over 50 years of operations, I studied for the 'Extra Class' operator's license, the highest class of operator's license the Federal Communications Commission license for an individual operator. My call sign now is 'W1QR' which signifies my class of license. Last night I talked to a man in Croatia and one in Turkey and another in Spain. I love talking to people in other countries and comparing information and notes.

In the old days, when television set used outdoor antennas, people would call my home and complain that "Your son is coming through our TV set loud and clear and if I would shut down for a while so we can watch our show!" This isn't a problem today, because our radios do not affect cable or internet TV programs. I must admit that at times, my wife would say she could hear me in the toaster oven, probably due to a loose ground wire!

I still continue to talk on the radio and have join in a contest know as Field Day. This gives us practice in case of an emergency. It is held the third weekend in June with different local radio club around the nation. We talk all over the world on emergency power and score points for the club. I also do all the cooking for the club members for the weekend when I'm not talking.

50 YEARS OF TEARS

It all began in 1962 when my mother read in the newspaper that Senator John F. Kennedy's motorcade was going to take a route right through Main Street of Marlboro, Massachusetts on his way to Boston. We all went down to the town common and waited, and then, amongst sirens and flashing lights, his limousine passed right in front of me. His window was half way down and he looked right at me and waved. I waved back and called out his name. He got out of his car and walked over to a ceremony. At 12 years old, and being in 6th grade, he was just an important person to me.

After grammar school, in 1963, I attended middle school, held in the old high school and was for 7th and 8th grades only. In 7th grade I was among those selected to recite the Gettysburg Address in front of the town for Lincoln's birthday.

My mother's family was speckled with Lincoln encounters. My great-grandfather from Maine entered the Civil War when he was 16 (he lied about his age) and was wounded by a Confederate baronet in his side. On his way home to Maine to recover, his train stopped at the Washington, DC train station. President Lincoln just happened to be there that day and he boarded the train to greet the wounded soldiers. When the President Lincoln came to my great-grandfather, who at 18 years old and only five feet tall, and had bright red hair, the President greeted him by saying, "Its young red-headed men like you who are helping us win this war for the union!" After being told this story for years, I felt I was obligated to honor both President Lincoln and JFK.

I remember very vividly the worst day of my young life. To this day, just writing about it still brings tears to my eye. November 22, 1963. It was a regular Friday afternoon in 7th grade, 7th period math class, with our teacher, Mr. Duca. At around two pm, our principal's voice came over the loud speaker with this announcement: "President John F. Kennedy had been shot in Dallas, Texas while riding in a motorcade!" Everyone was stunned and crying, even the teacher. It was the most shocking event of my life at the time. They let us all out of school early so we could be with our families and watch the tragedy unfold on TV. The media speculated about the event and two days later the accused assassin, Lee Harvey Oswald, was shot by Jack Ruby. To this day, there is a lot of speculation about what really happened during this tragic event.

On a lighter note, in 1963 I joined the youth group at church and we had sledding parties, church dinners, and hayrides and I was in a church play in front of 50 people with a fake mustache attached under my nose. I remember I didn't remember my lines but I got through it. Towards the end of 1963, I entered into 8th grade all ready filled with so much history.

GETTING THROUGH WINTER

As a young boy, winter was a time of playing outdoors and fascinations. We would slide down the backyard, make snowmen and wish for no school the next day. Building snow forts from the plowed up road snow was the highlight of winters. We would dig an entrance hole and shovel out a cave as big as needed to hold my brother and me. Mom would let us have a candle or a flashlight and she would make us sandwiches and treats for our caveman meal. Our dog, Holly, would sniff us out and try to get our sandwiches by pawing away at the entrance.

As we got a little older we were able to get shoveling jobs in the neighborhood. I always had to take up the slack because my younger brother was a little lazy, but we got it done. It was quite a feat to have earned some money from a real job. Naturally, the money ended up at the corner store where we bought candy. When the snow was real sticky we made snowmen and adorned them with carrots, branches and a hat or scarf. A bunch of neighborhood kids would walk over to the town common with our sleds and see who could go the furthest or fastest. Every time we would go there, our parents would warn us not to hit the trees in the common. We all survived winter and lived to tell these stories.

I joined the Boy Scouts and went on my first 'Operation Zero' hike. It was always in February, the coldest time of the year. We started off with a five-mile hike with our knapsacks full of food, tents, clothes and sleeping bags, etc. This was a lot for a 13 year old boy, but as I look back it was character building. We were to cook our food without pots and pans. We used sticks and wood splits for most meals and for breakfast we learned how to boil an egg in a paper cup with water. It worked! The fire would burn the cup down to the water line and heat the water to cook the egg. Amazing!

My first night in a tent was educational. We set the tents around the glowing fire to keep us warmer during the night. Some of the adults kept it going for a while after we were asleep. We slept two to a tent to stay warm and comfortable. We dressed in our sleeping clothes and eventually fell asleep by listening to the crackling of the campfire and the soft sound of the snow falling on our tent. In the morning, we got up and began to dress. But, we had left our shoes out inside the tent and they froze in the subzero temperatures! We had to put them next to the fire to thaw out before we could leave the tent. Now

I know enough to sleep with my boots in my sleeping bag. Being a kid in winter was fun and without great responsibilities.

As I grew up into adulthood, I had to shovel, clean my car off, plow, keep the house warm and travel in all kinds of winter conditions. I took up skiing but was petrified. I went snowshoeing and got lost and stuck; I smashed up a couple of cars and I was late for work and ran out of fuel. Winter was becoming a job, a four letter word.

After living in many properties in Massachusetts I moved to New Hampshire. Yes, north, where snow and winter lasted at least six months a year. I bought a 23 unit 1950's motel and cottage complex which had heat, hot and cold water running in pipes under ground between 11 cottages, with three furnaces between all of them. Yes, the pipes would rupture because of loss of fuel, corrosion and freezing temperatures taking down three units at a time. I can't count how many times I stayed up all night fixing pipes, keeping units from freezing, and moving people around. It was not fun!

My birthday is in January and in New Hampshire, that means that all my cars had to get inspected. Everything bad happens to a vehicle in the winter because of pot holes, ice, snow and salt causing rust holes in the body and trying to start one's car in the frigid cold weather. Three years ago I moved another two hours north. You would think that I'd learned my lesson.

We now have a three-family house in Lancaster and I'm back to shoveling and keeping up with winter. I don't ski anymore and hate the winter cold. It costs over $800/month to heat the house and we freeze at 50 degrees in our apartment so the tenants can have unlimited heat. 'Something's wrong with this picture!' We stay in bed most of the time to stay warm (not complaining). I can't wait to buy a trailer and move to Florida where it is warm and I don't have to wear so many layers of clothes.

Now don't get me wrong, winter has some advantages. We spend more time close and cozy together in our cold house. Food doesn't spoil on the counter and no matter what imperfections you have on your car, house or lawn it will all be covered in white until spring. But best of all, snow and winter makes our lives slower and more appreciative of the beauty and the peacefulness of winter. One of these mornings I will wake up and the snow will be gone for another six months. Can't wait!

Everyday is a new day, and today, the sun is out bright, even though it is minus 33 degrees below zero! The air is clean, not much traffic and no lines at the local fast-food businesses. What shall I do today? I guess I should try to start my car to see if it will start. I haven't been traveling a lot of miles lately, so sometimes my battery does not get its proper charge.

Here is how I start my car on a cold day. One, get in, that is after trying to pry open the frozen door while praying that it won't be one of those days when you finally get the door opened but, it stay that way and it won't close so I have to keep one arm on the door to keep it closed so it doesn't open while I'm driving! Two, shut off all accessories to conserve power, and three, turn the switch and pray that it will start. I can remember my father telling me, "If it is going to be real cold the next morning, go and fill your tank up if you can!" "That the gasoline will displace the water and prevent a frozen fuel line." These days, we have dry-gas which is formulated to displace water with alcohols. I always carry a 6-pack in my trunk. "Thanks Dad!"

Between me and the tree, I think winter sucks. I hate wearing layers, stripping them off, putting them back on, coming into the room, taking your boots off, finding slippers, if you left them where you took them off, or forgetting something in my car and repeating the sequence. I'm tired before I do anything. But, I should be thankful for winter. Sometimes, the winter gets the best of me and all I want to do is cuddle up in my bed with my wife with the electric blanket on, sipping a drink and reading a good book. I'm lucky I can make my own schedule and not feel guilty if I feel like taking a day off.

JOBS AND CARS AND EXPERIENCES

How do you get your first paying job? A new employment agency opened in Marlboro and I went in to see what was available. Not having any experience, other than being a paper boy, mowing lawns and shoveling, I wanted a steady job. I was 16 years old and wanted a steady pay check so I could have some money in my pocket for a car or a date. Wilson's Employment Agency was my first stop. I filled out an application but at the time there were no jobs available that matched my experience. Mr. Wilson asked if I wanted to help around the office, clean, and empty wastebaskets... I said sure. After a couple of weeks they called me with a lead for a 'stock boy and janitor' for a local stationery firm, Wilmore's. It would be my first steady paycheck, and I would receive $ 1.25per hour and would work about 10 to12 hours per week. Let me see, that's computes to $12.50 to $15.00 per week.

At my first 'real' job I was attentive and diligent but it didn't take long to get into the grind. Every job has its drawbacks and mine was to pick up after the owner. Mr. Wilson would walk around the store to see if there was anything out of order while he smoked in the store. It was my job to sweep the aisles and pick up his cigarette butts. I watched him throw them on the linoleum tile floor, crush them, and walk away. It always bothered me that he did this. My other duties included stocking shelves and empting waste baskets.

My father bought me my first car for my graduation in 1968. He paid $75. It was a 1959 Rambler four door sedan. We painted it blue using rollers and brushes and some paint he had left over from a house painting job. It looked pretty good. As it was in 1968, the era of 'flower-power' times, I added vines and flowers to the rocker panels on both sides of the car. You may not know this about Ramblers, but the front seats folded all the way down horizontally. It was great for parking or the 'submarine races'. Once, I took the car to an away football game and the clutch went in it, and I had to have it towed home, and eventually I junked it as it would cost way more than Dad paid for it to fix it.

My next car was a 1957 Buick Special that belonged to my neighbor. It was a big car, but the brakes weren't the best. I found out about another job in the next town of Southborough, Massachusetts working in a body shop. Finally I had a job where I could learn about fixing cars. During the summer, I did dirty work like sanding, sweeping, washing, sanding, sweeping but during this time, I asked tons of questions and learned all kinds of tips and procedures. I worked all summer and made some good money.

One afternoon, I was tooling around in my Buick with one of my friends and while talking away, I went through a stop sign. I hit another car, spun around and hit a hydrant and ended up with the whole drivers side of my car crushed. The other person was okay but he had to have his car towed away. I was able to drive my car, the 'Tank', home and it sat unrepaired on the street until it went to the junkyard.

My next car was a 1957 Chevy four door sedan. This was a good car. I bought it for $45 from a ham radio operator I knew. I drove it for about two years. I decided that I should learn how to fix my own cars so my next job was also in the automotive career. I pumped gas, and was a technician helper at an automatic transmission garage operated by two Portuguese brothers. One man spoke broken English and the other just nodded his head and laugh at anything I said to him. We all got along well and eventually, I learned how to remove transmissions and tear them down so they could be rebuilt.

Everyone makes mistake when learning a new skill, sometimes with mishaps. The first mishap occurred when I was helping my coworker disassemble an automatic transmission. Automatic transmissions are full of levers, clutches, linkages, gearings and locking rings. We were disassembling a shaft which had a locking ring on the shaft. He motioned to me to take a small sharp awl and place it in a hole to release the ring while he held the shaft. Well, it slipped and the ice pick shaped awl slipped and went right through his finger and out the other side. He took a rag and placed it on his finger and looked at me with a smile and shaking his head that said "It's OK." I thought I would get fired but I didn't. My other job at this shop was to pump gas at 25 cents per gallon and check oil and fluid levels as well as tire pressure. Sometimes a pretty girl would come in and I'd fantasized about the two of us as I pumped the gas.

I learned more and received more responsibility. We would go to junk yards and strip transmission parts out of junk cars and sometimes I would go on my own. One time I needed some rear shocks for my old Chevy and went to my favorite junk yard. There I found a great pair of shocks in a junk 1957 Chevy Convertible. I got most of the bolts off except one and decided to use a torch to heat up the stuck bolt to loosen it. I was careless and the convertible top caught on fire with me inside the car, and it went up in flames. I had no problem escaping. We had to get a backhoe and shovel dirt on it to smother the fire. The fire went out but the shocks went with it also. Another lesson learned the hard way.

Another day at the transmission shop, I was working on a big, four door, black Caddy, which needed the transmission taken out for repair. The first step in removing the transmission is to drive the car onto the lift rack and remove the driveshaft. Driveshaft's typically have four bolts securing them, two you can get to and two you can't get to unless you turn the drive shaft. I removed the two easy bolts and positioned my wrench on the hidden bolt and pulled down to rotate the driveshaft to remove the bolts. I guess I had forgotten to lock up the front feet of the lift ramp, and the transmission was in gear and when I turned the driveshaft the car moved forward, took on some forward momentum, and went right off the front of the lift and crashed into the wall and air compressor which was used to raise and lower the lift. I was in big "shit!" now. Well, needless to say, I lost that job. I lasted two months!

I learned how to fix the over 80 cars I've owned. I'm still working on my cars in 2019. We have five in the yard today. I completely restored my 1926 Chevy Landau sedan which had been a disaster which I drove for over 20 years, and my 1962 Austin Healey Sprite which I purchased for $400 and came completely apart in 12 boxes and a rolling chassis. This took me 1200 hours to complete and I still drive it today!

I next worked at a new food supermarket, Wonderful-market they newly build in town I took a test and got a job as a bagger, after another test I moved on to being a cashier. I worked there three years on and off to save money for college. It was a very family orientated company with parties and events for the employees. My brother just reminded me about a switch that was located on my left side and was used to turn on and off the rubber belt that moved the groceries to be processed. I used my knee to move it and over time and repetition, I developed water on the knee. My knee became very sore and I had to wrap it and wear a padded brace. This ended my part-time job career except for a trash collection company, because I just wasn't strong enough to lift the trash barrels over the side of the truck in the speed required to complete the route.

After college I had three electronics jobs behind me. The first was an electronic technician for Lincoln Laboratory a division of MIT. I spent 10 years there and they put me through school to finish my BSEE from University of Massachusetts. I was hired to build and test communication systems for satellites. I was lucky to go to the testing of the systems before their launch.

I continued to work for MIT but after the launch, MIT opened a new department developing low cost, practical Photovoltaic power system using solar cells. I designed test equipment to match and compare the systems. MIT received another grant from the Government under the Department of Energy under President Jimmy Carter. I was in charge of the first Residential Photovoltaic test site which consisted of 10 buildings put up by different solar companies to test their systems, solar cells and mounting systems that could be built as a retrofit or original as-built power system. I did the testing, made the equipment, gave tours, maintained the systems and wrote technical manuals for each system. I was lucky once to meet Charles Duncan, the Secretary of Energy under President Carter.

Eventually, a few employees decided to break away from MIT and start their own solar energy company, TriSolarCorp, and they asked me to leave MIT and work for them to head up instrumentation and field installations. So I did! They received a bid to build a photovoltaic power system to run a jack pump that pumped water from 600 feet beneath the earth in southern Arizona for the Papago Indians. Originally, the pump was powered by a diesel engine that had to be manned to operate and had to be shut off when the storage tank was full. Being a one-of-a-kind system, I was in charge of developing, building and installing the instrumentation to monitor its efficiency and dynamics of the system. I also developed a radio controlled switching system that signaled the power system to shut off when the tank was full. It was a success. All the instrumentation was mounted in a hollowed out fiberglass Porta-Potty. The Indians had a great laugh about this because they said, "I was the first white man to wire a 'head' for a reservation!" Ha, Ha!

Another time I had an interesting surprise while inspecting some equipment for my employer. I was sent to Massena, New York to look at a piece of equipment for a solar installation to be installed on a floating buoy in the Saint Lawrence Seaway. The day before the inspection, I decided to take a ride around to see the sights. I came upon a hydro dam in the seaway, which had a museum on the second floor. I decided to go to take a tour. You could look down through the floors where giant generators were located and see all the switching and distribution equipment in operation. This was my first time in a place like this. In the middle of the museum was a roped off raised platform area with two red felt chairs and a plaque that read, "In these chairs Queen Elizabeth and Vice-President Richard Nixon signed a working treaty to provide hydro-electric energy to Canada and the United States." To my astonishment, I was the only one in the museum. I looked all around but didn't see anyone or any cameras. I decided that this was my chance to be silently and secretly connected to these two people of famous and historical figures. I snuck under the gold ropes between the gold posts, and I first sat in Queen Elizabeth's chair, and then Richard Nixon's chair! I wondered if anyone else had done it before me; This made my day!

The next day I began inspecting equipment at a business. My boss had said to be thorough, get down on my knees, and look it over very carefully. I did, and on my way up from my knees, I struck a hidden metal bracket about a foot above my head. I caught it right in the top of my head! I hadn't been given a hard hat and now there was my blood all over the place. They said they were sorry for not giving me a hard hat, and took me to a local clinic where seven stitches were put in my head. I went back and finished my inspection.

Again, I was contacted by some of MIT engineers who left to work at Mobil Energy Corporation and they wanted me to work for them as a System Engineer. I developed testing equipment and also was in charge of New Product Design. I developed a packaged solar kit that could be mounted anyway and used to run electrical equipment for the home owner or small business. It was called, "The Blue Ribbon Kit" and was featured in Popular Science magazine. Mobil Solar was a photovoltaic cell manufacturer and they needed equipment developed to utilize their cells. I also worked on a portable high powered photovoltaic power system that came completely disassembled and fit into a 20 foot shipping container. It was then sent to Saudi Arabia to power a 100 foot tall lighting system for a major round-about. I spent time over there installing it and doing testing. I also worked on solar powered desalinization systems along the Red Sea and solar powered billboard lighting systems. It was an adventure in itself...I was arrested for illegally parking my car, took a shower with four naked women at a house party, ate lamb brain pizza, got chased by a camel, and learned some different languages. I stayed at the President of Mobil Oil's compound with my own driver where I had a man that took my food orders and had them ready for when I returned from the field and my own private swimming pool and car with a driver. They didn't let me drive; anyways, I would not think of it, because the cars while at a traffic light with only three lanes would stack up across the road seven or eight vehicles wide all beeping their horns! Jokingly, I said that the national bird voice of Saudi was the 'horn'! Inside the living room of the compound, the walls had a silk-like fabric walls and a canapé on the ceiling shaped like a colorful tent. On the way home, I stopped in Amsterdam. Yes, I visited one strip show in the red light district!

"The lessons I learned from these stories are: you can have great plans and good intentions but they don't always work out the way you expect them to. "Go with the flow" as they said in the '60's and adapt, enjoy, and apply your gained knowledge to everyday life to enrich your being. You never know when your knowledge will pay off, or, save your life or someone else's life!"

Printed in the United States
By Bookmasters